Telling Your Story, Building Your Brand

Telling Your Story, Building Your Brand

A Personal and Professional Playbook

Henry Wong

BUSINESS EXPERT PRESS

Leader in applied, concise business books

Telling Your Story, Building Your Brand:
A Personal and Professional Playbook

Cover design by Jessica Hui

Interior design by Exeter Premedia Services Private Ltd., Chennai, India

First published in 2022 by
Business Expert Press, LLC
222 East 46th Street, New York, NY 10017
www.businessexpertpress.com

ISBN-13: 978-1-63742-285-4 (paperback)
ISBN-13: 978-1-63742-286-1 (e-book)

Business Expert Press Business Career Development Collection

First edition: 2022

10 9 8 7 6 5 4 3 2 1

Description

In this new world, everything and everyone is a brand. People in business and careers recognize they have to work on their brand but seldom know how to achieve it. Just becoming known is not enough. Gathering social media followers is not enough. Standing for something is everything. In this book, branding expert Henry Wong shares his process used for product and people brands to compete in the market and workplace.

Most people typically can't afford the fees of branding firms. This book will provide access and insights into Wong's experience. It's ideal for entrepreneurs and professions in any industry looking to manage their business career. This book is more than just the theory behind personal brands. Taking an in-depth approach, it delves into such areas as understanding the personal brand, steps to creating one, as well as taking your brand to market. Part step-by-step guide, part story-sharing Telling Your Story inspires readers and helps them bring their own brands to life.

Keywords

personal brand; entrepreneurship; career building; brand storytelling; storytelling; brand guide; brand building; self-branding; marketing strategy; business management; branding yourself; professional branding; personal brand coach

Contents

Acknowledgments

If it takes a village to raise a child, so too, a book.

To my family—Donna, who tirelessly read and proofread excerpts and chapters, and Brandon, who helped research key points and pushed me further. And to my mother, and my father now passed on, who raised me in the back of a Chinese restaurant and taught me resilience and to see the good in everyone and everything.

The good thing about a printed book is unlike an awards speech, there is no orchestra or mike drop to cut me off. So, to my mentors, colleagues, and friends, Alex Pozidis, Atin Gupta, Chris Bryce, Dave Altomare, Harold Gerlach, Halcyon Tan, jc Molina, Jerry Philip, Joe Lu, Michelle Flynn, Pam Panesar, PY Chu, Sarbjit Kaur, Scott Boumeester, publisher Scott Isenberg, Tracy Ho, and Vince Gambino, who helped, encouraged me, shared their insights, and cheerleaded me on to this point, thank you.

Interestingly, I'd also like to thank Google. If I had attempted to write this book prior to their existence, I would not have been able to, without access to a universe of knowledge. Their suite maintained my notes and documents, gave me access to them anywhere in the world, and kept me generally organized.

And finally, gratitude to the guy in the audience at one of my talks who came up to me and said, "I should write a book." Here it is.

Introduction

Like many children of immigrant parents, I struggled to find my identity. I was born in Canada but was I Canadian? Was I Chinese? Or, Chinese-Canadian? How I viewed myself was often determined by how others viewed me. I grew up in the back of a Chinese restaurant. When I became of age, which in a traditional Chinese family meant when I could walk and talk, I did chores, I looked after my toddler brother. And then I worked in my family restaurant. By the time I was 11, I began losing the last vestiges of any Toisan accent that originated from a county in Guangdong, China, and was thrust into working behind the counter of the diner. I learned to take cash, calculated change backward, while engaging with truckers and families alike for who chop suey was their exotic foray into another culture. I talked. They talked. I told stories. They laughed. I could steer and adapt a conversation depending on the "audience." Little did I know this would inform and shape my own personal brand in the ad world.

After 30 years in the business, I've had fun times working on big, global multinational brands such Toyota, P&G, Johnson & Johnson, and Sylvania. I've had the opportunity to work on small, local, and startup brands. Last count, like anyone who's been in this business for these many years, I've amassed experience on well over 100 brands.

Years before that, I was approached by a political group who asked if I could apply my thinking to a candidate of theirs to help create a brand around him. I thought about it and realized that the same principles applied. I could use the same process to help define and tell his brand story. Since then, I've helped personalities, execs, and professionals develop their brand. Sometimes as part of their company brand. Sometimes as a standalone entity.

I began to formalize these steps when I was once asked to present to the executive networking group I belonged to. I decided to talk about personal brands so the night before, as often with homework assignments, I put together a PowerPoint outlining the handful of steps I used in creating a personal brand. I outlined my thinking lacing it with stories of real-life examples. My 30 minutes seemed to be a hit. One of the members asked me to speak at her conference. I agreed. The conference talk also received positive responses and more invites. One participant was kind enough to say you should write a book. Thanks, but talking is much easier.

But the thought did stay with me. Though I've delivered the talk dozens of times, a book would make it accessible for everyone. While company brands can typically afford agency fees to engage a brand thinking, many individuals can't. So, it's my hope for this book to provide that access to some accumulated knowledge and methods that you can apply to your own brand. Read on and tell your story.

SECTION 1

About Personal Brands

CHAPTER 1

You Are Your Brand

Or, why a personal brand is more important than ever today.

For many of us, we tend to take on the brand of the company we lead, we work for, and the groups we belong to. Whether it's being part of a startup, Apple, or Satan's Choice.

Why take on your own brand? Is a company brand not enough to define who you are? A personal brand gives you a competitive advantage over competitors and even colleagues. A personal brand helps you stand out. A personal brand adds premium value to your worth often monetized through promotions and salaries through perceived value. A personal brand is portable. You're not defined or limited by the organization's brand. You may leave the company to lead another or start another. But you leave with you, along with your file box of personal belongings, your brand. A well-defined personal brand if you so desire is influential and embodies the leadership qualities you have. As many consultants and motivational speakers have expressed, we are the CEOs of our own companies. The companies that are our personal brands.

Many aspiring leaders looking to establish their place in their universe often say, "I need to work on my personal brand." But what does that mean? For most, it simply means being more prominent, more well-known in their industry job or profession. But it's much more than that. Being known isn't a brand. Standing for something is. Being able to have a well-told story attached to you, even more so.

When we compare people brands to product brands, it brings this idea to life. Like every great brand out there, you're much more than just product features and benefits. From laundry detergent to cars to people, there may be a list of great attributes that the product has but there's only one you.

In the classic days of marketing, a Brand = promise + experience. You made a claim and you delivered on that promise. That's what established the brand.

Now a Brand = experience + storytelling. So, what do I mean by that?

A carpenter's son becomes a worldwide religious leader. A young millionaire engineer starts up a new car company that overtakes the big three. A celebrity assistant becomes one of the world's most influential personalities.

The ability to tell and share stories is far more interesting than the job title. And it's much more than the origin story. It's the ability to share common experiences and the openness for an audience to root for a protagonist that is the essence for every great story and every great brand.

Stories may have begun around a camp fire of our hunter and gatherer ancestors. And while the forum through such campfires as social media has changed, the connection to the stories and emotion is still the same.

Ultimately, a brand is a personal emotional connection with your fans or target audience. And in the world of competitive branding, it's compounded further—if you don't tell your story, someone else will. Silence can be filled by rumors and false tales. It's what PR people refer to as getting ahead of the story.

It's much more than controlling the message. The challenge for most people is that they don't know what their message is, never mind their story. This leaves their brand floating, without purpose or direction, with no one to connect with. This is the same principle in creating a brand story that makes for a successful connection with your intended audience.

I was a huge fan of "Monty Python's Flying Circus," a 70s British sketch comedy series with such great comedians as John Cleese. I remember this one skit in which Eric Idle as a TV talk show guest was teaching his audience on how to play a flute, "Just blow in one end and move your fingers up and down the outside." The same here. The process of building a brand can be deceptively simple. (1) Define who you are and what you stand for. (2) Define how that can connect emotionally with them. And (3), amplify it. Of course, if it was that easy, everyone would be doing it.

There are principles and methodologies that I've learned, developed, and, on the many product and personal brands, I have helped engineer. The deliverables were always the same. It came down to finding and creating the right brand story. However, it does require some experience (mine) and honesty (yours) to discover the insights, connect the dots, and express it. It's part art, part science, and part bullshit but all nicely wrapped up in a tale.

I remember a boss once telling me about reaching the top, likely from one of the many books he surface skimmed, that if by the age of 40, you're not at the top, near the top, or can't see the top, you'll never make it to the top. While there are many late boomers and early success is no guarantee of future success, this book is as well for entrepreneurs who has had to face bankers for financing, construct an organization of people, as well as build a customer base where they themselves are in the spotlight, and for professionals looking to stand out more in their organization. It's for those who aspire to build their image, build their success, and are looking for the tools to achieve that. By the way, Ray Kroc started McDonalds, Sam Walton started Walmart, well past 40.

I'm happy to share these principles with you in hopes that you can bring your brand, professional, entrepreneurial, or otherwise to life. So, you can tell your story and enhance your brand.

Let's begin the journey.

CHAPTER 2

Why a Personal Brand

Why you? Why you, indeed. Think of your favorite brand. What is it?

When I pose this question in my workshops, I inevitably get the same answer—Nike, Apple, perhaps a renowned fashion brand, or one of the car brands.

And when asked why they chose the brand, I often hear the same responses. It's the quality of the product or a technology feature or craftsmanship. A very rational justification of their choice. But then I press them further explaining that other companies make similar smartphones, other manufacturers make similar cars, and other people design similar quality shoes. At this point, most can't seem to fully articulate or give the reason why. They relent and admit, "I don't know why, I just happen to like it."

When we look at any premium brand, especially $250 running shoes, what separates one pair from another? When was the last time you remember buying a pair of Nikes based on their advanced technological cushioning? Or, their patented breathable waterproof material? You'll have to admit, it's all about your desire. That, and these key words: perceived value.

And that's the magic of a brand. A brand is more than a product or service. It's much more than just a logo. Many marketers used to say a brand is a promise—an unwritten agreement between the company and the consumer. Today, it's much more than that. Like Darwin's thinking, brands have evolved.

I once interviewed marketing guru, Seth Godin, author of *Purple Cow* and *All Marketers Are Liars*, in his Hastings-on-Hudson home office, a mere 17 miles but about an hour-and-half drive from Manhattan. We spoke at length about his theories and the one that he often espouses was: "Marketing is no longer about the stuff that you make, but about the stories you tell."

I would say that the stories were always there. From the early days of sudsy laundry soap and tobacco-smoking Marlboro man, stories have always been there. And the master brands of today from Google to Coca-Cola through to Nike have always had built in stories, both real and manufactured.

But that's no longer enough. Storytelling is really the conduit to building a relationship with your consumer.*

---

*A consumer is defined as someone who consumes your brand—banker, employee, customer, or shareholder. Maybe, even your romantic partner.

The story is just the medium by which you create an emotional connection to your consumer. And by emotion, I don't mean the warm and fuzziness of it all. Human emotions run the gamut from anger to fear to happiness to desire and degrees thereof.

It's the feeling and emotion that you create for the brand. And masterful brands tap into those feelings to stir up reaction and connect you with them.

So, can a brand be a person? Based on that criteria of storytelling and relationship, the answer is, of course. The act of branding a company, product, or service is a way of personifying and humanizing that entity. As a human, you already have a head start.

If you work in an organization, likely the brand of the company exists and is sometimes pervasive through the culture of the workplace and outfacing interactions with your customers. But those who excel in getting ahead within the company often have a well-defined personal brand. Those stand out people stand for something. Sometimes separate. Sometimes meshed with that of the company's.

A newspaper, *The Globe and Mail* reported that typically women earned 75 cents for every dollar earned by men. In 2018, for workers paid by the hour, women's wages were 87 cents of men's dollars. The article observed: "The gap is presumably narrowing as women acquire postsecondary education at a faster clip than men, but it does not seem to be going away."

So, why is that? We can't deny there is systemic discrimination for both gender and race. It's not right but let's look at it through another lens. It is about perceived value. The price you ask for is countered by the price someone is willing to pay. The best brands set their price. They rarely discount it. Thinking of yourself this way is using the same economic clout of perceived value.

Many studies have reiterated that women have a harder time asking for pay raises. But that often applies to the majority of us. How many of us have felt underappreciated for what we are contributing? "I do the same job." "I do a better job." "I've been at this job longer." "I deserve a (choose one) raise/promotion/that job."

Truth is, you deserve it only if someone recognizes that and is willing to pay you for the perceived value.

And even if you're just a company manager, the boss/worker relationship is a brand relationship. You're the brand and your boss, your target audience.

There's another study from the University of California. Its authors, Zoe Cullen of Harvard and Ricardo Perez-Truglia of the University of California Los Angeles, did an in-depth analysis of some 14,736 workers in a commercial bank in Asia. They tracked what happened to workers when they had a new manager. They showed that men's career trajectories and pay improved significantly when they switched from a female to male supervisor when observed years later. "For women, however, switching bosses to either a man or a woman did not translate into higher pay."

It was all about what the authors called the smooze effect. The important conclusion was: "Schmooze or lose is the message from the new study, but only if you are a guy."

The good doctors found that the power of schmoozing provided a solid reason for why over one-third of the pay gap between women and men existed. Men tended to schmooze more. But what is this really? It's a type of socialization that is simply built on an emotional connection.

We see this in other groups. Schmoozing or bonding emotionally is not something many visible minority groups were as well attuned to. Growing up Asian, the common advice was: keep your head down and work hard. And you'll be recognized. But experience and people tell us this is often not the case.

You may have the value but it is the perception of it. That's the personal brand. Those who are in sky-high C-Level jobs know that negotiating the compensation package doesn't follow a set of pay equity rules. It's about perceived value.

This book isn't about changing that bias but helping you identify and presenting the best part of you in your marketplace. And in this marketplace, we live in a world governed by conditions that are often driven by emotions. This is true in the stock market as it is in the job market. As with every brand, it's not about the features and benefits that you might have. It's about that emotional connection that you can form with your consumer.

With all things being equal. It's this perceived value that makes the difference—your brand.

CHAPTER 3

What Makes a Brand

Nibblin' on sponge cake
Watchin' the sun bake
All of those tourists covered with oil
Strummin' my six string on my front porch swing
Smell those shrimp
They're beginnin' to boil

Wasted away again in Margaritaville
Searchin' for my lost shaker of salt
Some people claim that there's a woman to blame
But I know it's nobody's fault

Don't know the reason
Stayed here all season
With nothing to show but this brand new tattoo
But it's a real beauty
A Mexican cutie, how it got here
I haven't a clue

"Wasting Away In Margaritaville." To understand your brand, let's take a look at what makes other brands successful. Did you read the lyrics above? Did your mind wander off to some beach-side bar?

How about the lyrics to this song?

Aruba, Jamaica, oh I want to take you to
Bermuda, Bahama, come on pretty mama
Key Largo, Montego, baby why don't we go
Oh I want to take you down to
Kokomo, we'll get there fast and then we'll take it slow
That's where we want to go, way down in Kokomo

Yes, another beach song by the group that defined beach songs, The Beach Boys.

Both are successful Top 40 tunes that you'll find play and sing along to on any pop Spotify playlist.

But what is it about Margaritaville that makes it special? It's more than just iconic for reasons that defy logic. I'm having a hard time recalling other songs by Jimmy Buffet. How is it that this one-hit wonder, if that is the case, reportedly earns $100 million every year? It's not from the royalties to his song but from what we refer to as his brand extensions. There are beers, clothing lines, hotels, restaurants, planned retirement communities, and oh yeah, his performing tours. Margaritaville is not just a song, but a state of mind and a lifestyle embraced by fans called "parrotheads" who long for a place that only exists in their mind or in Buffet's products. It's shared values and experiences. Being part of the Margaritaville brand is embracing not just a lifestyle but a mindset.

The best brands are never simply about the product features. There's a movement behind it. A belief system that has been created. In this case, it's what Jimmy Buffet and Margaritaville stand for.

The flip side shows a darker, more dangerous view of powerful brand movements. Taylor Swift fans, Swifties as they are called, relentlessly bullied the actors from the Netflix show, *Ginny and Georgia*, when she was offended by a joke retort from one of the characters. "What do you care? You go through men faster than Taylor Swift."

But as we go deeper, we see these brands have common traits. Their purpose and what they stand for is singular and focused. They are consistent and unwavering in their stance. They are believable at least to their fan base. And they often defy logic even when they're not logical.

A successful brand forms an emotional connection (satisfies an emotion). And for those who have a slavish following are often referred to as cult brands.

CHAPTER 4

The Entrepreneur's Brand

"I" Incorporated. Not every entrepreneur is an attention-attracting personality like Elon Musk or Richard Branson. The personal brand of an entrepreneur need not fit this mode. While true, many entrepreneurs have similar traits of being driven and passionate about their business, entrepreneurs come from all walks of life and personality types. They may have the defined hard skills of business management, leadership skills, financial management, marketing savviness, and strategy and planning. And while they have worked hard on creating their company brand, few have focused on creating the business brand of their own self.

But for those looking to raise capital, lead a company, a sharp look at your personal brand is one of the tools in that box that can inspire confidence in your role. But why? Just simply being the boss or having a well-detailed financial plan isn't enough to convince others to follow the leader. It is you as the brand that provides that added inspiration and confidence that turns the leap of faith into an easy step forward.

In the world of cycling, one of the most respected names is Colnago, an Italian bike maker whose history goes back to 1952. Founded by Ernesto, whose last name is, you guessed it, Colnago, the company became well known for its presence among professional cycling. So famous in the European race circuit, that it became an event when he presented a custom-made, gold-plated bicycle to Pope John Paul II. Each bike has two recognizable icons. A clover like that found on playing cards and his signature, which is a bit of an endorsement of his bike. And even though the company is now owned by an UAE investment company, the signature stays, reminding us of how people brands are as strong as the companies they represent.

The quandary for many entrepreneurs takes on added dimensions when it comes to their brand and the company's. If you're looking to sell the company that bears your name, do you sell your brand with it? Does the name of the founder of the company stay on as part of the brand image? Or, does it move into history? Or, is it just their philosophy and

founding principles that stay on? For many companies whose success is
so well tied to the founder, it can be a liability. How does the company
maintain its successful track if the founder is bought out or moved on to
greener pastures and no longer part of the day-to-day face of the company?

For those old enough to recall, rock icon Prince once went by a logo
that was a hybrid of the male and female symbol. At that time, people and
the music industry instead referred to him as the Artist Formerly Known
as Prince. It wasn't him being weird and clever, but a reaction to his record
label at the time owning the rights to his name and therefore the brand.
Although he did get the rights back, it underscored the sometimes tenu-
ous relationship between person and brand.

Many personal brands are the brands of the company. The antics of
Elon Musk define Tesla. The big O enthusiasm of Oprah defines Oprah
Winfrey Network (OWN). Zuckerberg and his hoodies set the tone for
Facebook. When the founder of the company has a very well-developed
self, the company itself forms a brand based on the identity of the person.

I have a client who is the CEO of an instant ramen company based in
South Carolina. Reza Soltanzadeh was once a medically trained doctor. His
first stint as a physician was volunteering in India for Médecins Sans Frontières
—Doctors Without Borders, where he saw malnourishment among the long
line of people who found their way into the clinic. While that was the start,
the middle of his story found him making his way to investment banking as
a healthcare specialist. Never forgetting that life of people he encountered,
he cofounded a food technology company that develops products such as a
plant-based instant ramen that has as much protein as three eggs. His goal is
to make the cost of producing this food inexpensive enough so that he could
make it available to developing countries.

His beliefs formed his story, and defined his persona. But was purpose
enough to form his personal brand? Having spent time with him, I know
him to be humble yet passionate. Super smart but not condescending. For
his company to hyper jump to the next level of success, it was important
to create more of a personal brand. He is a visionary though not readily
seen. He had to be the lightning rod for the movement behind the company and the product.

Those who do more than run a company, who instill their passion and
purpose into the DNA of their enterprise, are truly marrying the purpose
and the corporate mission into one brand.

CHAPTER 5

The Personal Brand Vs. a Company Brand

You are the company you keep. Or, are you? As a leader of a company, it's not difficult to exert your philosophy and brand on the organization. After all, it's your company.

But what if you're an employee.

How do you distinguish your brand from a company brand? Many people simply take on the brand qualities of the company they create. After all, as an owner, your company is often a reflection of what you stand for. Your own personal beliefs, the way in which you treat your employees, the way you conduct business are all you. But along the way, has that self been lost among everything else you created? Likely so, otherwise you wouldn't be reading this book.

Do you want to lead or follow? Stand out or stand in line? Standing out is as important to your career success as the hard skills you acquire. Being noted. Being defined. That's your personal brand working to help differentiate you.

A personal brand allows you to stand apart from the crowd and define what you mean to your audience.

Now let's look at how to do it.

SECTION 2

How to Build Your Brand

CHAPTER 6

The Audit

Time to hold up a mirror. In the process my firm applies to product brands, the first step is the audit. For people brands, it's taking stock of yourself. Assessing who you are.

When we complete an audit for brand clients, we assess the company and product in depth from customer surveys through to reviewing every aspect of their front-facing outreach like website, brochures, store experience. We speak to employees. We interview customers. What makes it a success? Or future success. What does the competitive field look like?

The idea is to have multiple lenses in which we are viewing the brand. It's looking at the brand from every direction. Inside, outside, all around. We do this because a singular look at a brand is not enough to gain a full look at the brand. Especially when that brand is you. Gaining a perspective of yourself through your eyes only is limited and very subjective.

You need an objective view. That could come from your colleagues, family members, business contacts, even the public. When we complete a brand audit in our work, we often do in-depth interviews to delve into what makes you, you.

It's a type of research. In marketing, there are generally two types of research—quantitative and qualitative. Quantitative research is a number-based assessment. It's a series of questions that at its basic level is a poll. 50 percent of respondents like Bob. 35 percent dislike him. And 15 percent are indifferent. It can get into aspects of his traits. 43 percent of respondents like his hands-on managerial style. 29 percent dislike his indecisiveness. A qualitative study provides more the "why" through in-depth feedback and statements. Why do you like Bob? What are the reasons?

The purpose of this work is to help gain some insights into what makes you outstanding. And how we can bring that to life. To do this, you will need some form of assessment to start.

I once met the head of a successful wellness product company. He had built up a brand loyal company such that when people, especially women, heard who he was gushed over him and his products. The interesting thing about him was that he built up a company of super ardent fans within his company. And he did this by using Enneagrams, a personality assessment tool that types your personality based on how you interpret the world and manage your emotions. It seems very EQ (Emotional Quotient).

His purpose was simply finding a certain personality type who would align with his corporate culture. He wanted to staff his company with other like-minded, loyal, fans who would be passionate about joining. Like many companies, it was a way of creating a corporate (cult)ure without the mind-control techniques. They come predisposed to his way of thinking.

A look at the personality types defined by Enneagrams yield some interesting archetypes:

THE PERFECTIONIST: Type One is principled, purposeful, self-controlled, and perfectionistic.

THE HELPER: Type Two is generous, demonstrative, people-pleasing, and possessive.

THE ACHIEVER: Type Three is adaptable, excelling, driven, and image-conscious.

THE ARTIST: Type Four is expressive, dramatic, self-absorbed, and temperamental.

THE THINKER: Type Five is perceptive, innovative, secretive, and isolated.

THE LOYALIST: Type Six is engaging, responsible, anxious, and suspicious.

THE ENTHUSIAST: Type Seven is spontaneous, versatile, acquisitive, and scattered.

THE CHALLENGER: Type Eight is self-confident, decisive, willful, and confrontational.

THE PEACEMAKER: Type Nine is receptive, reassuring, complacent, and resigned.

You could look at the list and select one that you think you are. In doing a test, the theory of course is that it gives a more accurate rendering of yourself. So, Enneagrams also have a wing which is at least one of two types that are adjacent to the dominant type; all very interesting especially when you look at some of the soul-searching multiple-choice questions.

I've often worried
  [ ] that I'm missing out on something better.
  [ ] if I let down my guard, someone will take advantage of me.

Much of my success has been
  [ ] due to my talent for making a favorable impression
  [ ] achieved despite my lack of interest in developing "interpersonal skills."

My
  [ ] reluctance to get too involved has gotten me into trouble with people.
  [ ] eagerness to have people depend on me has gotten me into trouble with them.

I have
  [ ] needed to show affection to people.
  [ ] preferred to maintain a certain distance with people.

I have liked to
  [ ] challenge people and "shake them up."
  [ ] comfort people and calm them down.

This is not a recommendation for a process but a look at some self-analysis. You can, however, look it up online or grab the book. Try a sample and see the results.

Now is this any different than a Myers Briggs personality test? The famous test developed by mother and daughter, Katharine Briggs and Isabel Myers. Their in-depth work started during the Second World War as a way of helping determine what jobs were best suited for them. The test evolved into its own brand and product, that is, the Myers-Briggs Type Indicator (MBTI) that has been the basis of determining employee fit for major corporations for decades. For the MBTI, there are four basic types that include introversion/extraversion, sensing/intuition, thinking/feeling, and judging/perceiving. And of this, there could be as many as 16 unique personality types.

If you took a Myers-Briggs test, you would have sat through questions like:

1. At a party do you:
    a. Interact with many, including strangers
    b. Interact with a few, known to you

2. Are you more:
    a. Realistic than speculative
    b. Speculative than realistic

3. Is it worse to:
    a. Have your "head in the clouds"
    b. Be "in a rut"

4. Are you more impressed by:
    a. Principles
    b. Emotions

5. Are you more drawn toward the:
    a. Convincing
    b. Touching

6. Do you prefer to work:
    a. To deadlines
    b. Just "whenever"

7. Do you tend to choose:
    a. Rather carefully
    b. Somewhat impulsively

8. At parties do you:
    a. Stay late, with increasing energy
    b. Leave early with decreased energy

9. Are you more attracted to:
   a. Sensible people
   b. Imaginative people

10. Are you more interested in:
   a. What is actual
   b. What is possible

And, so on.

And while some psychologists and scientists alike have deemed it unreliable because the same person can get different results when retaking the test, it can at least be the beginning to know yourself. And could it be that we are ever evolving and changing human beings?

I can't tell you what may yield the more accurate result. However, think of these as guides rather than complete assessments. This is just the beginning. There's your perspective. Their perspective. And then, the truth.

The audit needs to look at a brand through multiple lenses. So, try them out. It's only part of the picture of who you are. And not to be facetious but look up your astrological profile while you're at it. Multiple results are good in seeing where the commonalities are.

I had a number of people take both tests as a test. With some minor variances, it did seem to yield the same principle traits.

One final note on personality profiles. While it may provide a good perspective on who you are, it doesn't always provide a road map of who you can become. As a person, even as a brand, we have the choices to grow, evolve, change, and not be limited by what we are but what we can become.

Sociopaths as Brands

While we're on the topic of personality tests, one fascinating area of exploration and research is the number of sociopaths, people with antisocial personality disorders and perhaps even psychopaths who are leaders in companies and government. The traits are rather disturbing—manipulation, deceit, aggression, and a lack of empathy for others, many of which are well-hidden.

Surprisingly, one in five business leaders may have psychopathic tendencies. Or, maybe not so when you think of the bosses you may have had in your career. I certainly saw this in my industry and began wondering if advertising attracted a certain personality type at the leadership level.

Dr. Nathan Brooks, with Dr. Katarina Fritzon and Professor Simon Croom, is one of the authors of *Corporate Psychopathy: Investigating Destructive Personalities in the Workplace.*

I spoke with Dr. Brooks over a Zoom call to better understand whether some CEOs were serial killers under their corporate suits.

Dr. Brooks, a professor and forensic psychologist, with handsome surfer dude looks. With a friendly Australian accent, he speaks authoritatively on this topic. Based in Queensland, his research helped to create a spectrum of understanding with his *Clinical Classification Criteria of Psychopathy.* It's not so much a binary conclusion of whether certain leaders are or not a budding psychopath but the degree in which they are.

From his study, he describes them as "successful psychopaths— high-flyers with psychopathic traits such as insincerity, a lack of empathy or remorse, egocentric, superficial yet charming. But all under sheep's clothing."

"Certain personality types have learned to adapt and manipulate the way they present themselves," he said. "They have discovered instinctively how to connect with you on an emotional level. They have harnessed their personality or charisma to first lead and then control."

His book, *Corporate Psychopathy: Investigating Destructive Personalities in the Workplace*, makes for some fun reading. Along with his colleagues, he examined these Dexter Morgan[1] like personality traits in the corporate workplace. Analyzing over 1,000 corporate professionals, he came to some conclusions that were interesting.

One was that while one in 100 people in our community, and one in five people in the prison system are considered psychopathic, these traits are not uncommon in the top ranks of the corporate world, anywhere between three and an astounding 21 percent. Thinking back on

---

[1] TV character from a series called Dexter in which the titular serial killer hunted and killed murderous criminals.

some of the clients and bosses in my past, perhaps that number wasn't so surprising.

And two, that many companies may have their recruitment process a bit backward. "Too often companies look at skills first and then secondly consider personality features," Brooks says. "Really, it needs to be firstly about the candidate's character and then, if they pass the character test, consider whether they have the right skills."

To Dr. Brooks, "A lie is just the tool for them. What they say creates an image and a first impression. In the parole or the criminal sense, inmates with these tendencies before a parole board hearing are more likely to be released than non-psychopathic offenders. It's a very high-stakes situation where they are able to manipulate and influence the outcome. In some ways it's surprising that we don't actually see more psychopaths getting through the door in organizations because the simple demeanor is set up to really change and control how people perceive them."

On the other hand, based on how a personal brand does shape perceptions, it is how we form our perceptions of any one especially in that initial meet and greet, that first hand shake where you may be pulled in by the person's charm and charisma. While this may be part of their personality, it does shape how we are affected by them.

In the world where we do business, meeting company goals requires that confidence in the leader you believe will get things done and lead the company to success. We agreed that some of those traits are important for a leader, but there is a whole set of psychopathic traits that can be problematic. Dr. Brooks shared that "I think the simple answer is you need some of these, but you don't want too many."

Many of us have seen this first hand, where we've been witness to rash financial gambles and bullying, and thus creating a toxic work culture. Yet, those are often forgiven when quarterly results are met. We accept much for a return on that investment.

As a brand, if you find yourself on this outer end of the psychopathy, you may be concerned or with that lack of empathy, it may not even matter to you.

However, you determine your own assessment; it's a guide not in stone conclusion. Unlike popularity polls of politicians, your self-audit is never meant to be an exact science but a qualitative approach that gives you insights into the person that you couldn't get otherwise. It helps to form a picture.

Look at your performance reviews. What image does the media say about you? Your social media presence. Family. Friends. Colleagues. What picture is being formed of you.

It's all about self-discovery. Is it where you want or even need it to be? Is there an adjustment that might be needed to serve up your brand in another way? We'll go deeper into this with the next stages.

CHAPTER 7

What Is Your Purpose?

Let's go to the movies for a sec. "Your mission should you choose to accept it is to recover the stolen item designated Chimera." If you've ever wanted to understand a mission statement, look to any of the Ethan Hunt/Tom Cruise movies where he is given his mission before the recording self-destructs and sparks an exciting, thrilling adventure. It's right in the title of the movie, *Mission: Impossible*. A mission statement is a goal. It's a straightforward objective.

But it's not your purpose.

When Microsoft was founded, their mission statement was "A computer on every desk and in every home." I use this as an example to show the difference between a mission statement and a purpose statement. Unlike a mission statement, a purpose statement provides the "why." It's the reason for what you do. Ethan Hunt's MISSION is to recover the stolen Chimera to save the world (PURPOSE).

A purpose statement thinks beyond a mere promise. Brands are full of half-delivered and broken promises. It's not enough to simply set a goal. A purpose is your reason for being. What drives you? What motivates you? A variation of this is what people in my industry call a brand promise, your reason for existing, your reason for being.

Brands often look inward (some call it navel gazing) when they should be looking at how they connect with the greater world. That means looking beyond what you simply stand for and looking at your purpose. To answer the "why."

So, here are some thoughts that can help you understand what I mean:

- The most successful brands satisfy a need or desire, perceived or otherwise.
- Being the best, the most successful, the most innovative is not a true purpose. It's an objective that any person or company

can have. And for us human brands, such an end goal may be more ego fulfilment.

In many organizations, especially those that are civilized and democratic, group consensus often rules. Those of you who have participated in coming up with missions, values and goals, or in brand sessions, or Strength, Weaknesses, Opportunities and Threats (SWOT)[1] meetings or other group thinks, may have observed this one deficiency in the process. We typically allow every key stakeholder to have their say. We go around the table and have everyone provide their 3-cents. It creates this perception that each valued team member has an opportunity to contribute. The belief is that the approach ensures agreement of the mission statement.

The problem with multiple contributors is that in taking a phrase here and word change there, you get everyone's input, but the exercise doesn't truly align people. You get agreement on the message but not alignment.

Agreement is all about compromise.

Alignment is ensuring everyone believes the final words.

For your own brand, it is only you working through this exercise. What is the reason you exist? Why do you exist? What purpose do you have? Your purpose or reason for being should be clearly defined. By you.

When you observe the inner workings of the most successful brands ala Tesla, Facebook, Apple, and even old money brands like Berkshire Hathaway, you see there is one person, one leader who has a very clear vision and purpose.

So, while you can bounce your purpose off people around you, don't build it by consensus. You want to be clear in your mind. It should be near and dear to your heart.

Having a purpose is an articulation of not just your focus, but what you want to put your energy toward. To believe in something.

I was lucky through most of my career to not have to face that ethical dilemma of having to resolve what we sold versus what the hidden harm. The company I run today is focused on working with clients and people

---

[1] An analysis that takes stock of one's Strength, Weaknesses, Opportunities and Threats.

who truly have a desire to do business not just ethically but to better the world. A touch naive perhaps but the intent is sincere.

Of late, many ad agencies have guided their clients along this track, to follow purpose-driven marketing. Purpose becomes a marketing tactic. Standing for something like improving the environment is much more engaging than having resin in your chewing gum. And it does work, sometimes to great success.

Hellman's Real Mayonnaise got behind the real food movement. It was a focus on nonartificial food and food scarcity. Feminine product, Always, began redefining what it meant to run or hit like a girl. These are bigger movements than just the product. Can you be bigger than just you, the product? Can you stand for something?

What is it you are setting out to achieve? To make the world a better place? Improve people's lives? To do no evil, as once espoused by Google.

These examples of purpose statements are much more just clear missions.

IKEA is "To create a better everyday life for the many people."

For JetBlue, it's "To inspire humanity—both in the air and on the ground."

Lego thinks "To inspire and develop the builders of tomorrow."

And even Microsoft evolved to a much grander, much more inspirational, "To empower every person and organization on this planet to achieve more."

While there may not be anything concrete, the idea of the purpose statement is to create your motivation. It can be abstract. It can be high concept. How we fulfill it and make it concrete comes later.

A purpose is exactly that—it's your driving force. So, think purpose, not a mission. What need do you serve? What bigger picture can you help paint?

Wrap-up thought: A purpose is what you can give to others. It doesn't have to be in a nonselfish way. But what can you contribute to someone's life or on a higher plane, to society. So, start thinking in terms of a purpose statement—not a mission statement.

And for those still seeking to be the best, fulfill your purpose and being the best will follow. Need help getting started? I'll give you the first three words: "My purpose is …"

CHAPTER 8

What Is Your Superpower?

Bullet-proof skin. Instantaneous healing. X-ray vision. These are the superpowers found in comic books. What I'm referring to here is our own human powers that can make us exceptional.

Although you may think, "I'm not anyone special," at least think about what makes you stand out in a crowd? What do you excel at? Is it your powers of persuasion, strong observational skills, organizational abilities, high empathy, perhaps? I'm not a motivational speaker, but I do like to think that each of us has the ability to excel and be special. To be the best we can be.

Even being an entrepreneur is truly special. The metamorphosis from working for someone to working for yourself, whether by design, by accident or by no other choice, defines a unique trait. What drives it can be your superpower.

Let's look at understanding it and how to identify it. While in marketing, we call it your value proposition. I'd like to think of it as a superpower.

It's your "er." What is it that you can do stronger, faster, better? Temper it with a look at yourself. You may have an exaggerated view of yourself or you may have a lower interpretation of yourself. Is it realistic? Is it a true representation of who you are?

To get to that, go to your assessment. You should have compiled a list of attributes.

Get an honest validation from friends and colleagues. We do this on behalf of our clients. An objective third-party can often pull very honest, unfiltered answers from our clients' inner and outer circle.

There won't be any one method of finding yourself. On a board or post-it notes, write out each one. Hold up these traits. Which ones do you find are often repeated by people?

Form these in a hierarchy as shown in Figure 8.1. What traits are at the top? Which ones are the more honest assessments?

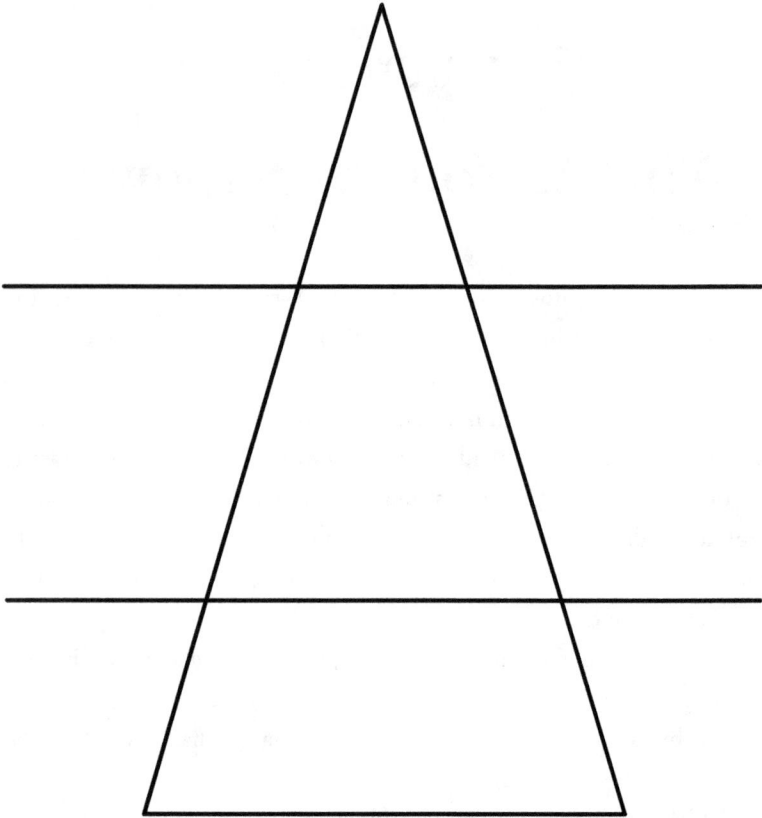

Figure 8.1 This is a simple hierarchical drawing I often use to rank attributes and keywords. There may be many descriptors of yourself but ranking them helps to assess who you may really be

Now take a closer look. Does it seem like a good superpower? Something that would give you a competitive advantage over someone else? That makes you stand out in a crowd? Is it something you want to be known for?

What happens if you find yourself just a mere mortal and human being? Each of us has the capacity to grow and learn and acquire skills or a superpower. Even the goal of wanting to improve can be a superpower. In Japanese culture, it's referred to as kaizen—continuous improvement.

Every season, I try to learn something new. From auto mechanics to Filipino stick fighting to mastering card tricks. I find ways of improving my capacity to learn and improve. None of these skills are my superpower. I'm good and decent at many things. I can't say I've reached Olympian level. But I would say that my curiosity is a notch above. I'm far more curious than most. This has led me to take on tasks or try new endeavors that I wouldn't normally. From rock climbing to technology, I'll try most things. Just out of curiosity. But it's also spurred me to be interested in people and my clients' businesses. This natural curiosity has led to that bit of success in my business. It's allowed me to be as well versed in the science of laundry detergent to alternate energy sources or even accounting practices. That's my superpower—the power of curiosity.

So, if you can't find your superpower, go discover one.

CHAPTER 9

Competitive Review

Seth Godin, the marketing expert I met on a project, authored *Purple Cow*, a best-selling marketing book. In it, he speaks about standing out, like a purple cow. How being remarkable is "worth talking about. Worth noticing. (being) Exceptional. New. Interesting." Counterpoints by others make the point that while purple cows grab attention and stand out among every other cattle, most brands want more than attention, they want sales.

For people brands, part of the equation is all about standing out in the crowd. To be noticed among your peers in not just a noticeable but in a meaningful way. Standing out doesn't lead to success but it's the first step.

What this means is that it's comparative. To stand out, you are assessed against others in your business or company.

So first, take a look at your competition. If you're in politics, it can be quite apparent. If you're in the work world, it could be your co-worker competing for the top job. If you're running a company, it's people in the same job, likely in a competing company.

For years, the public compared Apple's Steve Jobs to Microsoft's Bill Gates. Apple versus PCs. Making your personal brand come alive isn't just understanding your traits and superpowers but looking at who you are competing with in the marketplace.

Martial arts action star Jackie Chan recounted one of the reasons he became a mega success was that he stopped trying to be like the legend before him, Bruce Lee. In the beginning, Chan was trying to be the next Bruce Lee. But people didn't want the next Bruce Lee. And while many kung-fu flicks coming out the 70s had their share of bruceploitation films, they were like poorly made, knock-off brands you would find on the alleyways of New York. From a distance, it looked like the Coach handbag, but upon closer inspection, no.

So, unlike the many imitators of Lee, Chan developed his own style. Rather than have dangerous killer strikes and kicks and that unique cat scream, Jackie Chan developed a more clown-like buffoonery and Harold Lloyd-like stunts that wowed audiences in a different way. This is positioning. Finding a place in the minds of your audience that separates you from everyone else.

Back to your competition. You may need to stalk them, albeit in the professional way. Read through their profiles. What's said about them? What do they stand for? What are their features and traits? You can begin listing them. Positive and negative. What are the attributes of your competition? Do they appear to be more thought leading? More experienced? Less experienced?

On a white board or Post-its, write yours in a different color, including your superpower. Stick them up. And observe. What attributes separate you from them? Can you be distinct like Jackie or are you falling into a sameness trap. And to do that, like the cow of color, it's not enough to be remarkable, you have to do so in a way that's relevant to the people you're targeting. Here's where we take it further. Next up, positioning.

CHAPTER 10

What Is Your Position?

Knowing your mission statement or your purpose isn't enough. It's all relative. What distinguishes you from the competition? Positioning is the place you sit in the market. Or more so, the place you occupy in people's minds.

There are two aspects to positioning. What do you stand for and how you stand up against everyone else in the market. And knowing what you stand for offers a certain comfort of knowing your place in the world.

Look back on Apple versus PC commercials. There were a series of TV spots with hipster actor Justin Long, who always introduced himself with, "Hi. I'm an Apple"—in a side by side with everyman John Hodgeman, who introduced himself as a PC. The commercials were fun and entertaining but it not only positioned what Apple was, but it also repositioned what PCs were. Part of the success of these ads was that they didn't go after other computer manufacturers such as HP and Dell but the entire market. It became clear what set Macs apart from the world of boring beige boxes.

But the world isn't as delineated as Liberals and Democrats versus Conservatives and Republicans. We exist in a much more nuanced world.

To help clients understand these nuances, I use a series of charts mapped out with four quadrants. Each end of the axis is labeled with key attributes. To do this exercise, look back at the words you have accumulated for both you and your competition. Look for two sets of words that should be polar opposites of each other.

Examples might be:
Methodical | Free-thinker
Process driven | Big picture thinker
Humorous | Serious
Introvert | Extrovert

Team player | Leader
Physical | Cerebral
Empathetic | Self-focused

And so on. Choose the two sets that can represent your persona.

To understand the exercise, look at the example in Figure 10.1. This one is made up of Linear versus Creative; and Casual versus Corporate. You will have your own set of attributes.

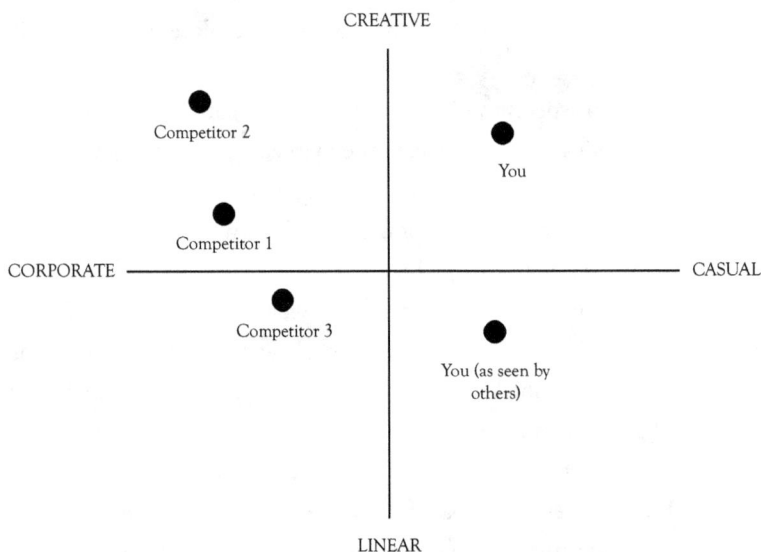

Figure 10.1 Use a positioning chart with your own labels to determine not only how you see yourself against competitors but how you see yourself as an brand

Part one: On the quad chart, place a dot or a small Post-It Note® in the spot that your competition may sit. What space do they occupy? Are they more creative yet corporate? More corporate but linear?

Part two: Now place a dot where you might occupy. Are you creative yet casual? Throw the dot up there. Most of us are degrees of key attributes. The quadrant spaces allow for flexibility as to what your position will be. A bit more casual? Move it more so along that axis. However, looking at the other axis of creativity and linear thinking, you may see yourself or wanting to position yourself more creatively.

Part three: This part of the exercise is how your target audience might see you. Invite input from a colleague or friend who has enough insight and understanding of you to place a dot. (Provide them a blank sheet without your own dot to get a more, objective, unbiased view). Don't be defensive or offended if you are looked at differently than the way you see yourself. The goal of this exercise is twofold. One, to see how you stack up against competitors. Two, see how you are being perceived by others. If there is a gap between you and the competition, good; you potentially have a good position to stand out among the others. However, if there is a gap between you and how your "consumer" might see you, some work is needed. It means that you need to alter or shift that perception to close the gap.

CHAPTER 11

What Are the Reasons to Believe?

Why Should I Believe You? Back when I worked on Proctor & Gamble (P&G), the makers of Tide and Oil of Olay, I was so entrenched and accepted in their marketing process and machine that the client allowed me a blue security card that get through all kinds of doors to their inner sanctum. Trade secret leaks and unwanted visitors were kept at bay by P&G's building security.

As their creative ad agency, we would present outlandish and sometimes brilliant creative ideas. None which would see the light of day. P&G always took a very logical linear approach. A+B = C. If we made a claim, it would have to have a "Reason to Believe" (RTB). Or, as the marketing team called it, an RTB. Tide could make a claim that they could provide the whitest whites because there was a key ingredient, an enzyme in their formulation which they called carezyme. Carezyme was a chemical which would react to the food or stain molecules on your clothes without affecting the fabric. In the world of laundry detergent, this was revolutionary. But more importantly, from a brand perspective, it provided the proof in the pudding stain. Or, a way of removing the pudding stain. This was the reason to believe.

Resumes are a perfect example of a communication medium that is often fraught with little reason to believe. I'm not a career consultant but the principles of branding still apply here whether you're writing a resume for a job or a bio for your profile. Here are the common phrases you may have written:

"Works well independently"
"A great team player"
"Results driven"

"A hard worker"

"Good communication skills"

"A fast learner"

"Strong attention to detail"

Sound familiar? Many of us make these unsubstantiated claims or simple self-observations, which are not only what others would type out but share little in the way of helping me believe what you say.

If you make a claim, it can't be an unsubstantiated one. You need proof points, substantiation, RTBs, or evidence. It's referred to as delivering on your brand promise.

Often, this begins with your education and work experience. Go back to your resume. What does your LinkedIn history look like? Does it support who you want to be and the story you want to tell?

This is the exercise:

Start with the claim and then the support and proof. List all the RTBs that can back your claims.

Here are some examples:

Strong organizational skills (proof: "initiated and oversaw transition to new project management software that helped to manage workflow on over 30 client files").

Strong leadership qualities (proof: "managed a team of 4 sales executives that effectively grew revenue 10 percent in the first two years." This one should be easy to prove or not; either you manage a team and lead or not). In the absence of actual experience, you may have taken courses or leadership training which is still a reason to believe.

Effective communicator (proof: "delivered a series of workshops on being an effective leader").

While you may not need to spell it out in great detail, you do need to have the backstory to support your claim and for others to believe in it.

Final thought: Also look at the claim itself. Are these what are often called table stakes; the price of entry; what others offer? What is the big unique claim that you can make? And can you prove it?

The Halo Effect

Back in the 1920s, psychologist Edward Thorndike coined the phrase, "halo effect." It was really a term he used to describe a type of bias we have in our initial perception or judgment of someone.

The idea is that our assessment of that person is based on some other attribute. See a beautiful blonde woman dressed in tight-fitting crop top and jeans; we may think of her as being sexy but dumb. A well-dressed, suit-adorned man; we may see a successful business person. A foreign person in their native attire; well, you come to your own conclusion. The point is that we are influenced by first impressions. Thorndike, used the term, not only to describe the phenomenon, but to prove that we are often wrong in our assumptions.

Over 100 years later and we still fall prey to our cognitive bias. I remember a bit by comedy great George Carlin as he described the arrest of a killer. He mocked the neighbor, the woman who kept saying, "but he was such a nice guy." Our perceptions often don't match reality. The halo effect has shaped often wrongly, sometimes correctly, our perception of a person's character or intelligence or competence. And studies since Thorndike's continue to reinforce this bias from teachers judging students to waitresses getting higher tips to inexperienced people getting promotions and raises based on their attractiveness.

So in marketing, I use this term in another way. Ever name dropped? You know, used someone else's name to make yourself look better? Product brands do this consistently, especially when the brand may be lesser known. Intel Inside wasn't just a famous tagline but a way for lesser-known computers to use the more known entity of Intel to gain customer confidence. An unknown Chinese brand could be confidently purchased because of the Intel sticker that appeared on the laptop. Any celebrity endorsement from Brad Pitt for TAG to Jennifer Aniston for Smart Water uses this halo effect.

Recognized companies you work for, your industry memberships, the schools you attended are all halos which can cast a positive light on you. And are tools for you to enhance your brand.

CHAPTER 12

The Six-Word Story

Story has it that author, Ernest Hemingway, once bet over several shots of tequila, that he could tell a story in six words. On the napkin, in the Havana bar, he wrote, "Baby shoes. For sale. Never worn."

I do a similar exercise for my clients. It begins in group sessions with multiple stakeholders at the table. We set out sheets of paper and markers and crayons. And I ask them to tell their company brand story in six words. Add a doodle if you like, I say. It's often met with long pauses and some head scratching. "How many words?" "It's not possible." I give them 10 minutes. And it yields a wide array of answers. Some brilliant. Some not so much. But it gets them to focus on being concise, thoughtful, and sometimes creative. Mostly, it focuses them on that key message.

It's no surprise that this assignment yields a wide range of adjectives and nouns, and various expressions of thought. But rare do I get that full alignment in which everyone's six words are alike. What it usually demonstrates is that the organization needs help in telling their story, consistently and with focus.

Building a brand is all about a single-minded message. After all, what is the one thing you want people to think of when they think of you? So, take this same challenge: Tell your brand story in just six words.

This is an exercise that leads to your key message. It can be one sentence or a couple. It can be just a list of words. Or, a complete story. These six words which if you can write effectively capture everything about your brand and can even help provide that needed competitive position.

Here are some examples from my workshops.

"We bring the world's weather inside."
"Education from the heart and mind."
"Our health for one another. Together."

And for people brands:

"Globe trotter brings new world perspective." (global marketing director)
"Once homeless. Now finding people homes." (real estate agent)
"I never forget it's your money." (financial advisor, of course)

If you as the driver of your own brand can capture the words in six, you create a simple message that everyone can accept and follow. It isn't a compromise. It's knowing what your brand stands for. And it can't be nebulous. It has to illustrate what your brand is all about.

Fellow brand experts and many attuned clients often declare that a brand message should fit on a billboard. That is, if you're driving by a billboard, you should be able to read it easily. Yes, the six-word exercise does that, but it's not the word count that counts. The six words is more than just a box to confine a story. A great six-word story, like Mr. Hemingway's, allows the reader's imagination to fill in the blanks and connect with them on a deeper emotional level. Good to be concise but don't forgo the deeper emotional connection.

CHAPTER 13

What Is Your One Word?

After you do the six-word exercise, and you have an array of traits, can you boil it down to one single word?

When I say Volvo, what do you think of? Or Apple?

Each of these masterful brands have created a brand so strong, you immediately identify it based on one single attribute.

Like a Zen master would say, when you can describe yourself/your brand in a single word, you truly understand yourself.

To get there, do this next exercise. Write down all the single words that describe you. These are words you may have used on your resume, that is, key words that have come back from your own assessment. The way others have described you. In following a similar approach for clients, we pour through a brand's website and marketing material, our interviews and compile a list of these words. And sometimes, it can be extensive. When there are words that are repeated, we begin to circle them. The more circles, the more likely it will be that one word. We discuss. We debate.

Your list doesn't have to be extensive. In fact, the shorter the better. But do the same. Circle the ones that repeat themselves. Typically, the word that is most circled is your one word. Now is it? Take stock. Does it reflect who truly are? Does it reflect what others say about you? Can you come to a conclusion objectively?

What is the one word you can own and stand behind? Is that what you stand for? Can it define you?

CHAPTER 14

What Emotion Can You Satisfy?

We've talked about emotions and its importance in forming your personal brand connection with your audience.

The best brands try to satisfy an emotion and be a conduit to some well-placed feelings. Take a look at some of our favorite brands. Nike—the desire to be the best. Volvo—safety for peace of mind. Coke—happiness.

Robert Plutchik was a psychologist emeritus professor at the Albert Einstein College of Medicine. How could you not be a well-regarded profession with the mention of Albert Einstein (halo effect) in your resume? Plutchik was known to be gentle and wise with a sage-like manner. He was what many consider a pioneer in helping us understand emotions. Vulcans likely evolved their ability to free themselves from emotions based on first understanding them. One Star Trek reference permitted here. Professor Plutchik created a Wheel of Emotions (Figure 14.1) that organized eight basic emotions based on the physiological purpose of each. You can understand the effect this would have in all walks of science and sociology.

The primary emotions are eight sectors that showcase eight primary emotions: anger, anticipation, joy, trust, fear, surprise, sadness and disgust.

And there are the opposites. With each primary emotion comes its polar opposite. These are based on the physiological reaction to each emotion.

The eight basic emotions in this theory are:

- *Fear*
- *Anger*
- *Sadness*
- *Joy*
- *Disgust*
- *Surprise*
- *Trust*
- *Anticipation*

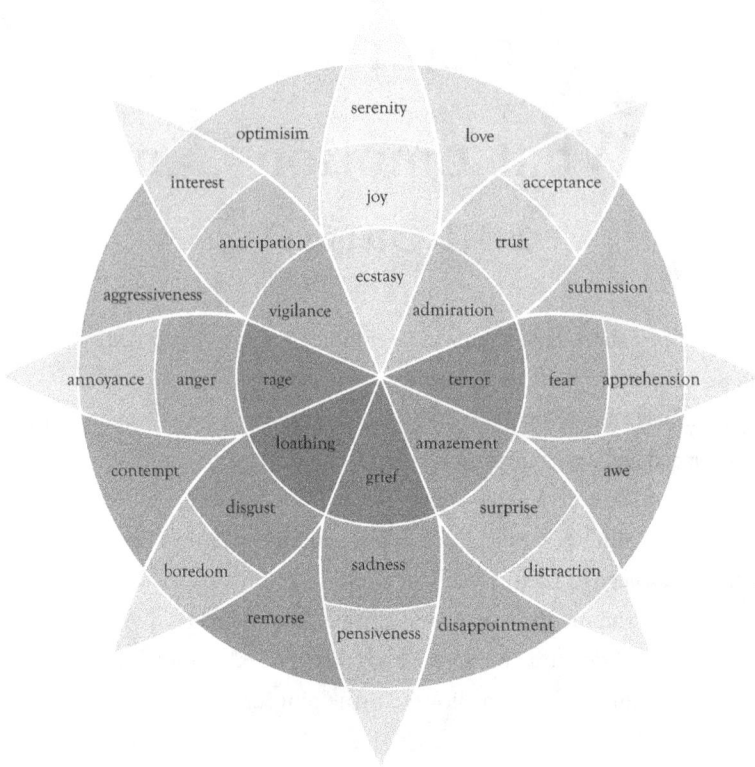

Figure 14.1 Plutchik's Wheel of Emotions in visual form

And looking at the combination of emotions along the wheel has helped academics and song writers alike understand intense feelings.

If we look at the more positive ones that brands want to sit in, these can be limited.

If there is a wheel of human emotion, there are also degrees of each emotion. We know emotional feelings aren't binary, on or off but degrees of intensity. Think of any satisfaction survey that immediately appears in your inbox after interacting with any customer service of any food delivery company or online bank where you are asked to rank your level of satisfaction. One being very dissatisfied and 10 being extremely satisfied.

Consider this as you do your own self-analysis. Trust can be peace of mind. Assuredness, confidence can be fairly neutral. It doesn't stir your emotions but it's not a negative reaction. Joy does move the needle. Joy is what most brands aspire to provide you in the form of excitement or appeal. But what about other descriptors like satisfaction, happiness, security, confidence, assurance, calmness and so on. This may be the feelings that you want to trigger in the people you lead, collaborate with, or even persuade.

One common trait sometimes observed by my clients is that level of calmness I apparently exude. The emotional feeling that comes from it is one of comfort, perhaps peace of mind on the part of the recipient. It's not what you might project but what is perceived and received that shapes the emotion.

In other relationships, what happens when emotions such as love run so intensely that when not satisfied, it causes an equal and opposite reaction? Emotions can be manipulated. Jealousy can cause hatred, on the one end, and desire, on the other end. Emotions can be complex. Fascinating as the Vulcan Spock would observe.

It doesn't have to be direct emotions but simply a human need that you satisfy. It's more than a checklist. So, what is the emotion that you can satisfy? What type of emotional support can you provide?

You don't need to play with people's emotions but you should understand what emotion you can provide. Understand that and you'll see how it's an essential start to a meaningful relationship.

CHAPTER 15

What Is Your Brand Personality?

Your personality isn't just a list of traits. It's the effect you have on people. What is the relationship you have? For entrepreneurs and business leaders, the brand is ultimately the relationship and connection you have with your circle of consumers, vendors, partners, and even staff.

It's the effect you have on people that is your brand personality. Brands are ultimately relationships formed in the minds of consumers. So, what is that relationship you have with your consumer, colleagues, or constituents? By understanding the emotion you satisfy, you can understand the personality behind your brand.

Working in the ad industry, there comes a certain archetype. They're the Don Drapers[1] of the world. Jonathan (I use this fictitious name but this describes countless people) was a colleague of mine. We worked closely together creating some amazing ad campaigns. To fuel not just his courage but his ability to socialize, he depended on alcohol. Or to reverse the words in a more clinical way, he had an alcohol dependency. Unbeknownst to me, at first, he would sneak shots of whisky before meetings. He explained it away in a sincere and meaningful way. He needed it to not give a damn whenever he presented or had to speak to a room of nodding heads around a boardroom table. I could see how these situations would be intimidating. At the time, it seemed like a plausible answer. Compound this with the level of serotonin that's created in the adrenaline rush from presenting and getting a $1,000,000 campaign approved and you can understand how the feeling is addictive. Or, becomes addictive. You never want it to end. Soon, he needed it just to interact with people. Or, get through the day. I see now that it's part of the personality of people like my colleague.

---

[1] Don Draper is the hard-drinking, womanizing ad man character in the AMC series, Mad Men.

Here are my thoughts on charisma.

I can't tell you how to be more charismatic. I'm not that kind of guru. While there are countless books and workshops that are happy to take your money and share those insights, I will provide a brand perspective.

People with charisma are attractive brands. If you look at some of the tips that are taught, many of which go back as far as Dale Carnegie's "*How to Make Friends and Influence People,*" you can look at it through the lens of a brand. The commonalities are there. Charismatic people focus on you and make you feel like the most important person in the room; they make you feel good being in their presence; they tell good stories that connect with you. So too with brands.

Brands that do so are humanized in a way that if they were human would be considered very charismatic. Let's look at my statement again: Charismatic people focus on you and make you feel like the most important person in the room (*targeting*); they make you feel good being in their presence (*emotional connection*); they tell good stories (*brand narrative storytelling*) that connect with you (*relevant messaging*). That sounds like good branding to me.

While you may do a makeover to fully rebrand yourself while improving on your social and emotional skills, you are still matching your brand to an audience. Like a product, just make sure that this audience is who you are wanting to target. Your brand and personality may not be the light that everyone gravitates to. But it's you at your most authentic. Brands find their audience. And perhaps your audience may not at all be interested in Michelin-level cuisine but is very happy with steadfast, reliable diner food.

CHAPTER 16

What's Your Story?

You're at a networking event (at time of writing, it was in the form of Zoom calls) and as you meet people, the deer in the headlights question often comes up. "What do you do?" "Or, tell me about yourself?"

You have now been officially put on the spot. This is even more amplified in a business networking event and the Zoom calls (akin to appearing on broadcast TV) where you would have had 30 seconds to a one minute to tell people about yourself.

You've been asked to provide your elevator pitch or, in personal branding terms, your story. The pressure and stress for most of us is palpable.

So, what is your narrative?

"I worked the last ten years in sales for a packaged goods company where I lead a team in selling to the specialty retail market."

"I started in the family printing business and then I helped grow the operation to a franchise across the country."

While I sort of made these up to protect the guilty, words of such have often been the reason for suppressed boredom on the part of your audience, whether one or 500. It's not to say that these individuals are boring; it's to say the way the story is told is much less interesting than one more carefully crafted.

If you've stumbled or rambled when asked about yourself, you're like most who really don't know where to start when it comes to talking about yourself.

First, let's understand why story is important. The ability to storytell has been essential to the survival of society and humankind.

In his book, *Sapiens*, author Yuval Noah Harari talks about the power of storytelling in not just bringing humans closer together, but for our survival. Gathering a tribe with a common belief system shared by story creates a common bond but essentially keeps everyone in check.

We've seen this throughout history where storytelling pulls people together.

In his movie, *Braveheart*, Mel Gibson as Scottish rebel William Wallace, delivers a rousing speech that motivates his army to go to battle. It's a film, but the same storytelling techniques have inspired generations of people throughout history to take up arms, give up their freedom, or work harder and more tirelessly. Sift through Winston Churchill's orations and you'll find the same. Prefootball game pep talks, definitely. Cults, yes. Startups, for sure.

A number of years ago, the doorbell rings. I answer it and a young lady stands on my porch, slightly wet from the rain. She explains that she has just moved into the neighborhood, down the street by the corner. As luck would have it, her car just got towed. She is beside herself, upset and near tears. Then she asks if she could have $100 to get her vehicle out from the pound. It was a good story and I showed empathy but not sympathy. The more she went on, the less believable it was. Add to the fact that I had heard this story years before but pitched to my much more sympathetic father. Back then, his hand was already in his pocket reaching for his wallet by the time the sad soul who rang his door spoke of being towed.

As an ad man then and now, I am a moderate cynic. In this situation, my only reply was, "I'm sorry, I work in advertising, you can't fool me." Instead of shock, the young lady just smiled and walked away. No protest. No counter-argument. Funny how that line works so well against robo-calling telemarketers and scam artists looking to free you from your money. But the young lady and countless con artists know how the power of a good story could potentially connect with people on an emotional level and persuade them to donate to their cause.

Believing in a cause is fundamental to motivating people. The story is just the conduit to that motivation. Employees who believe in a cause work for less. Or for nothing in the case of charities and political campaigns. Why else would people volunteer? Most of us believe in some cause but a story shapes a belief system and gets people off their couch to do so.

A story helps you illustrate a point. It provides the reasons to believe. It connects emotionally with people. It is the medium by which you connect with people, to persuade them, to enthrall, inspire, motivate. And pay for their $100 towing fine. But without structure, it's not a story but a rambling monologue. Without structure, audiences lose the sense of what you are pitching.

The best pitches, whether spoken or written out in an email, are those laced with elements of a well-constructed tale that are often made personal.

Creating the Structure to Your Story

To put it together, we begin with a long-form structure. This will provide the basis for all other uses. Every story has a beginning, middle and end. Seems obvious, but this basic structure is often lost when you are asked to provide that proverbial elevator pitch. Does your story meander? Do people's eyes glaze over as you share your surgery details, and talk about your first job out of high school? It's more than being relevant, it's taking your audience on a journey. We'll get to that shortly. Looks like I'm meandering.

Once Upon a Time

The best brands have a point of origin. Nike waffle shoes. Garage PCs of HP.

It's all about the story. I once helped to create a small brand archetype around a microbrewed beer, called Dead Elephant. The beer is made by a brewery in St. Thomas, a small southwestern Ontario town about two hours outside of Toronto. It was here around the turn of the last century that the famous PT Barnum Circus came to town. One of the featured acts, Jumbo the elephant, was tragically struck by another train while being disembarked. Legend has it that he died while saving the lives of others. This became the inspiration for the Indian Pale Ale.

We actually included that story on the beer can and it became part of the design. Unlike packaging, most brands, personal or otherwise, can't have a story appended to the product. You have to rely on a logo and visuals and mnemonics. You have to rely on other ways to share your uniqueness. Your story.

Looking at the top-grossing movies of all time, among the most popular genres in movies today is the comic book story. From *Spider-Man* to the full-out *Avengers*. The back story has always been a key element in creating sympathy for the superhero. Everyone has one. Ant-Man is a petty thief who wants to be a better father and human being. Peter Parker is an awkward high school teen who is driven by the guilt of not being able to save his murdered uncle. Captain America is a soldier whose inner spirit, if not outer body, was focused on fighting for democracy. Batman is driven by the grief and anger of seeing his parents murdered.

Walking a short mile in a character's shoes gives you the connection to them. You sympathize with them. You empathize with them. You root for them. You're now vested. What are your origins that may connect well with people?

So, ask yourself, what is your origin story? How did the version of you today begin?

Understanding this is important to what your brand represents. As I have said before, if you don't control your story, someone else will.

But how do you put a story together? That has often been the struggle of people trying to enact their brand.

Clients selling from one business to another (aka B2B aka business-to-business) have at times engaged my firm to write their case studies. It's their proof and narrative of a job well done. But, "We're struggling with it. Can you give us a hand?"

Business cases are profiles which provide a product or service and want to show other clients and customers the story of how they helped one of their customers so they can show how they can help the new prospective client.

The structure of these case studies is often overlooked. It's quite simple, really. And we map it out this way. One) What is the background of this situation? Two) What was the problem? Three) What did your company do to solve this problem? Four) What were the results of the solution?

Your Own Case Study

In putting your story together, it's very much the business case of you.

What are your origins, your background that has led you here? What situation or trigger prompted you to follow the path you're on? What did you do to fulfill that situation or solve the problem? What success led you there?

Let's look at it another way that may help you form your story. It's the structure of a movie. There are few of us who don't enjoy a good movie and the story that is told.

Your Story

There is often a setup that tells the backstory of the main character; there is a plot point that sends the character on their journey. All seems to be well until a major obstacle hits them in the face and all seems to be lost. The plot point often triggers a problem or situation that sends the character into a tailspin that needs to be solved or resolved. Then in the final act, the protagonist overcomes that life's roadblock to typically live happily ever after.

Most popular movies follow this to box office success. It's true. Look at the top list of all-time movies. It includes *Avengers: Endgame, Titanic,* and *Star Wars.* Even smaller and yet no less powerful films follow this. Formulaic? Perhaps, but it works in Hollywood. It may be great CG effects and acting par excellence but it's the story that movie goers love. The beginning, the journey, the conflict and the resolution in the final act that enthrall people.

Notice a common theme? This is a narrative format that has existed in ancient Greek tales such as Homer's Odyssey. And is often referred to as the hero's journey. The hero's journey is a style so ingrained in our tribal connections as humans that it's been said to even predate religion. I would go further to say it likely helped to brand religion.

First, you have a character that you establish in the early parts of the story. In your movie, how are you the protagonist? How does it play out? This structure focuses on one main character (you) and how you grew through the trials and challenges you faced.

Humble Beginnings: The Start and Inspiration.

Mark Zuckerberg was a well-educated computer hacker and programmer who left Harvard during his sophomore year to create Facebook leaving a trail of lawsuits to become one of the world's richest media magnates and now philanthropists.

Oprah was born into poverty and, in pursuing a broadcasting career, latched onto hosting a small-time Chicago talk show that, with her exuberant personality, transformed her into one of the most highly rated daytime hosts which was the catalyst to her becoming one of most influential media and cultural personalities on the planet.

Steve Jobs was a college dropout who with Steve Wozinak began building computers in his garage under their Apple brand leading to huge initial success followed by excommunication from the company before being restored to CEO and leading it to become the largest company on the planet.

Richard Branson was a music record salesman who formed a chain of Virgin Records stores and molded a multitude of business under the Virgin brand and his brash stunts and showmanship including music studios, airlines, mobile phone service, and hotels.

And before you think that these stories are simple to write because of the happily ever after ending, you should know that these narratives have been deliberately shaped as much by me as the people themselves.

People and likely history will gloss over the fact that Branson had a failed Virgin cola, car, publishing, and clothing businesses, as well as a past that includes tax evasion charges. Or, that Steve Jobs had a therapy-rich personal life of adoption, birth mother reconnection, and his own unacknowledged daughter.

Controlling the narrative not only shapes your story but that of your entire personal brand.

You might have also noted that I wrote these short narratives as a single sentence. I was once asked to deliver a talk on mentorship. In these usual instances, you're asked to provide a bio. The request was for it to be two sentences "or so." I looked through my files and found a number of them that I use depending on the need. None of them were two sentences. Had I been guilty of the same verboseness that I try to get my own clients to curtail? Perhaps. I do know, it's definitely a worthwhile exercise to be able to pen a single sentence of your own.

The long stories of Homer, Luke Skywalker, or Oprah are examples of the hero's journey.

But instead of a long tweet, let's use a long-form block. The story is very much like a sculpture. An artist begins with a large piece of stone or marble and in a manner of speaking and chips away at the inessentials until they are left with a beautiful work of art. Your own two sentence narrative needs to start with its own big piece of marble.

CHAPTER 17

The Story Structure

Time to look at how you can map your own story structure.

Here are some tools that you find helpful: giant Post-It® notes. Recipe cards. A whiteboard. Or maybe you just want to map it out on your laptop. When I rented my latest agency space, I was genuinely happy to see glass partitions between offices. Not for privacy but the fact that I could use dry erase markers to write on its surfaces. Capturing thoughts in big form and being able to stand back and look at its entirety helps with the thinking process and in our case, brainstorming. So, too with your brand.

There is another tool that marketing agencies use. It's a briefing document. For creative work and for project assignments, it captures the essence of everything that you want to achieve in a campaign. The background, the single-minded proposition, the research, and the human insights are captured on a document page and laid out for the team to wrap their creative and strategic heads around. The trouble I found was that the brief was seldom brief nor insightful. It often became a dumping ground for everything the client shared and sometimes confused more than elucidate. So, I began just using a series of questions that if the strategist writing up the brief could answer, it could be the brief we needed. So, following that same process, use these questions to help capture your storyline.

What Were Your Beginnings?

It doesn't have to start with your childhood. But it should start at the point that had an influential or profound effect on your personality or growth. Did you grow up in the back of a Chinese restaurant? Did you have an alcoholic father with whom you had to move 17 times by the age of 16? Did you grow up bullied and your father got you into cart racing as an antidote? Were you a singer in the church choir before writing and singing songs with your brother?

Who/What Was Your Influence?

How did your beginnings have an effect on you? What was the catalyst to your journey? Was it early Junior Achievement days? Was it selling chocolate bars door to door? Maybe, it was having a Mr. Miyagi type mentor in your life?

What Did You Learn?

These could be the life lessons. The inspiration or the drive that propelled you forward. For many, it's a common story of living with less that motivated them to do more. To reach their level of success.

What Was The Major Obstacle You Faced?

Sometimes the bigger, the more disastrous the event, the more dramatic it can be. Good story but it can also be as minor as identifying a simple problem. The molehill doesn't need to be a mountain. Before Apple became the trillion-dollar company it is today, Steve Jobs was booted out of the very corporation he started. What was the event or problem you faced?

How Did You Overcome It?

It may not be you-centric. Perhaps you were part of a team. Perhaps someone rescued you. But you can still be the main character in your story.

What Was The Success?

This can be easily answered because there is often a measurable achievement attached to it. If it isn't, retrace and find another story path.

What Did You Learn From It?

Is there a life lesson from it? What did it teach you that you can share with others?

How Does This Make You The Unique Individual That You Are?

I am here as I am today because …

What Is The Benefit To Others?

Bring it back to the people you're targeting. A product that has key features needs to have a benefit attached to it. So too, people brands. A local politician's son was forced by his parents to help out at the food bank. His exposure to those less fortunate shaped his empathetic approach to winning voters in his journey to the governor's office. But on a less grand level, perhaps you may have worked in a warehouse stacking crates of frozen pizza. The idea of rolling-up-your-sleeves hard work is now second nature and part of your teamwork approach.

As you answer each question, the sentences become a short or long paragraph to your story. But it is long form first. Later we condense into shorter versions.

Would you ever make use of this full story? Perhaps as a biography. This is more of your self-analysis. It's unlikely you would publicly share this long script. It's an exercise to get you to understand your own journey. The script to your movie. It gives you a deeper understanding of who you are. The key insights and foundation of you as a brand. If you were to go back and review the audit of yourself, how does it compare?

Where this can be used more is as components and parts that help you fine tune your narrative and its different uses. The About Me page on your website; the short intro on social media, the pitch deck and, of course, the elevator pitch when meeting people.

After you write the narrative, try the six-word exercise again and see how that has evolved.

A couple of last points to keep in mind: Tailor your story to your audience to make it relevant to them. How is it interesting to the people you are pitching to? And is there an emotional hook? You formed the content but don't forget to forge a connection to your public.

CHAPTER 18

Using Your Story

Where can you tell your story? In an interview. In a meeting. At a networking event. All those situations where you are typically asked "so tell me about yourself."

Today, meat labeled free of growth hormones and antibiotics are quite commonly found at the grocery meat counter. I once worked on a brand called Maple Leaf Foods. Their brand of chicken began including a line, "raised with antibiotics." When that concept was first introduced, it was so well accepted by consumers that it led chicken sales, even with its premium price. Sales now claim more than 44 percent[1] in some markets. But by advertising their meat was free of antibiotics, it suggested other brands weren't. They didn't need to do a competitive side-by-side comparison. In a simple announcement with a sticker on a meat pack, they told discerning shoppers that their competition was likely inferior.

Your use of storytelling can effectively reposition your competition. A brand story that is more interesting shows a unique you that can make competitors seem less effective and less engaging. You don't have to trashtalk or criticize the other guys. Your consumer can draw that conclusion. In telling your own story well, you can suggest that what is out there is lacking.

The Elevator Pitch

Let's revisit this with what you may have picked up.

The average person speaks about 100 words in a minute. No one will time you for that 30 seconds. Can you tell your story in 100 words or less to provide an engaging pitch?

I was once at a networking event. There were well over 25 to 30 people. The structure was a bit more unusual. It was a rapid fire of each

---

[1] OCO. 2019. Premium Meat Market Study.

person, members and their guests, standing and delivering their company pitch. What they do. What their company was all about. As everyone went through their intros, some long, some short, some meandering, some clear, and some muddled, I realized that my elevator pitch would be lost amongst all these people. After close to a half hour of hearing everyone deliver their minute monologue. I changed my approach and stood up and said something along the lines of: "Hi everyone, my name is Henry Wong. While I am one of a gazillion Wongs in this world, I happen to run a branding company. I help companies and their leaders tell their story in the marketplace. But I'm here to hear about yours—to meet some great, interesting people, which I have already. I know this is a business meeting, but I enjoy anything on wheels like cars, road and mountain bikes, motorcycles. If you want to grab a few minutes to chat about that, I'd be happy to meet and even if you don't, it'd still be happy to meet you."

It worked for me because it reflected my style and my personality. It's not necessarily a company pitch, though it was. It wasn't my life, but it did provide a bit of my family history. But the more important aspect was that it opened the door to more meaningful chats with people. And it wasn't about the transaction.

For that, I got a chance to meet a handful of people, who found me engaging and disarming. I told what I do, I connected with people emotionally by sincerely complimenting them on being interesting, and I disarmed with my background. I established a quick memorable trait about my interest which moved potential discussions from being just about a transactional business (after all, why would anyone want to do business with you just because you show up at a networking event. It requires a longer, more meaningful discussion, which I opened people up to). I changed the basis of the conversation.

On another Zoom call, I was a computer screen away from people. In it, I was concerned about again being lost among the many pitching. A key rule in branding—stand out. Not for the sake of standing out. But in a relevant and meaningful way. So, I did a show and tell, bringing samples of products I had worked on holding up cups of ramen, toy cars, Tylenol packs, and other samples that I had on hand.

Some final pointers to keep in mind even as you put together yours based on the outline.

You wrote your story out, don't read your story. Tell it like you would to your neighbor.

Avoid the intricate details of being too technical. Perhaps, people in your industry may be interested. But leave that deeper discussion for when you actually have a meeting with people or prospects. Don't get too personal. Unless it's relevant to your brand and can help you connect with your audience. Your elevator pitch isn't the final destination. It's the start of a more meaningful conversation.

CHAPTER 19

Creating a Mnemonic

For a personal brand, a mnemonic can be a visual symbol, a name, a physical characteristic, or some association that acts as a way to help define or recall you and your story.

A mnemonic isn't your brand. It's the thing that represents you. But deeper than that, it's a short-cut to presenting your personal brand to the public.

So, you can have a better understanding of how a mnemonic can fit in your professional life. Let's look at the ways in which you can use a symbol or a hook to represent your professional persona.

The most visible way is a visual representation. In the world of branding and design, this is your logo. It's how people can tell one brand from the other usually through visual cues.

The word branding came from American ranchers using hot irons to burn their symbol on cattle to mark their ownership. Others say brands began as far back as the early days of British pubs that used symbols of such names as Cock & Bull or Fox and Fiddle to communicate names to illiterate but enthusiastic ale-drinking customers. But the use of symbols as a form of communication can be traced back further to cave drawings. The use of iconography to represent key ideas has been long with us.

Some go as far as creating a wordmark based on their name. Their symbol becomes part of their signature on a card or e-signature. However, most of us typically don't go around wearing a logo emblazoned on our clothing, even if your name is Calvin Klein or Donna Karan. Although those who watched afternoon reruns of "Laverne & Shirley" will remember Penny Marshall's swirly embroidered "L."

The best logos are those that represent traits or aspects of the brand and have a story behind it.

It's no wonder brand symbols have become so fiercely protected. While people don't typically have a logo the way a company brand does, let's look at ways in which a person can utilize a symbol or mnemonic to represent themselves.

If a mnemonic can be a trigger to recalling the person as a brand, it doesn't always have to be a carefully crafted symbol.

Apple's Steve Jobs was known for his black turtleneck and khakis. Hong Kong director Wong Kar Wai for permanently worn black sunglasses. These were their mnemonics. Those cues became their symbols. But unlike disgraced Theranos CEO, Elizabeth Holmes who strangely copied Job's dress code, these outward displays usually represent their personalities. For Jobs, wearing the same thing every day eliminated one daily decision so that he could devote his mind to other things. For Wong, he said he could never think fast enough and the sunglasses allowed him that needed pause in front of people and his actors as he formed his thoughts.

A mnemonic doesn't have to take on a physical form. It can be an idea.

I had a colleague whose first adventure was crewing on the yachts of the likes of Bono and other well-heeled people who could afford weeks at a time on the sea with all the luxuries of a personal staff, chef, and crew. There was a way in which life was on the boat that formed her understanding and insights of people. Her success today can often be traced back to the hierarchical chain of command on a boat, personal interconnections, seeing different cultures in different ports around the world, and managing up her bosses. Her whole brand could be ascribed to everything she learned on a boat. If she had a book, it could be titled, *Everything I Learned About Business I Learned On The Ocean.* That was her mnemonic.

I also once helped a sales consultant whose education background was Zoology, which is very different from helping corporations with their sales process and strategy. His hook was his understanding of animals and how they could be personified as humans. By categorizing different target customers according to their animal personality, we had a way of presenting his unique process. That was his mnemonic.

It can also be an expression, physical or verbal. There was a certain trope that ran through TV sitcoms in the 80s. A main or secondary character had an expression that when trotted out would elicit the laugh track. The Carleton dance in "The Fresh Prince of Bel Air," JJ Walker's "dyn-o-mite!" from "Good Times," and Janice's chortled laugh from "Friends." Those were their signature mnemonics.

CREATING A MNEMONIC   73

What's yours? Wearing vintage watches because you value time? A never changing hairstyle that represents your consistency? Colorful socks that represent your fun character? A verbal expression captures your mission? What reflects you as an individual that you can use as your signature?

Remember your brand isn't defined by your mnemonic, your logo, or even your name. It's defined by your story behind these tools. If you choose to have a mnemonic device, have it reflect your personality, a trait. Give it some meaning. What is the story behind it? What can represent you in a relevant fashion? That's the way to symbolize and reflect your brand.

CHAPTER 20

Naming

Branding companies like mine are paid what seems to be outrageous sums of money to come up with brand names for companies and products. The work itself isn't in the name itself. It's in the work leading up to it: Hours of research, trend analysis, stakeholder interviews, copyright exploration, and the naming process itself.

For you, should you change your name or have a unique moniker?

Some brands need to change if they need to reposition themselves in the market. U.S. cable network, American Movie Classics, which started cable TV life by showing classic black and white movies like *Citizen Kane* became AMC to rebrand itself from old movies to new original programs like "Mad Men" and "Breaking Bad." Company brands often need to do this as there is brand equity (some call it baggage) tied with names.

Other companies change their name to separate themselves from the personal brand of the founder.

As a name in the history of brands, Apple shows that you can be called anything. Names seldom describe the core business but instead light up the imagination of their target customers.

In the movie *Batman Begins*, Bruce Wayne says, "As a man, I'm flesh and blood, I can be ignored, I can be destroyed; but as a symbol … as a symbol I can be incorruptible, I can be everlasting."

And if we were to take this further, as a personal brand, names don't necessarily define who we are. The exception seems to be in entertainment. The story is indeed different.

Would one of the world's most beloved rap artists be who he is if he was known just as Aubrey Graham? Nora Lum aka Awkwafina and Stefani Joanne Angelina Germanotta also known as Lady Gaga. And the list goes on and on. In entertainment, your name is your brand.

It used to be, to sound like you were part of middle America, you would have a middle American name in a bid to have greater mass appeal.

If we have evolved, it's that we try to reflect our roots. We embrace our unique backgrounds. Or, we redefine ourselves.

Many of us simply adopt our middle name. Few of us do a complete overhaul of our moniker. Names are very personal. But if you are looking to shift to a new label, ideally you want to ensure it reflects your brand traits. And likely you've had this conversation with yourself before you have thought about your own brand if you have thought about a name change.

In the end, you can call yourself anything. And be remembered by it. It's not the name that defines you. It's what it stands for and your story and your persona and what you deliver that ultimately defines you.

CHAPTER 21

Bringing Your Brand to Life

Studies vary but the wide-ranging general consensus is that we are exposed to 5,000 to 100,000 messages per day. Seems an exaggerated number but walk through your day and you'll see what I mean. Between magazines, Google ads on every web page we visit, social media ads, billboards, TV ads, radio or podcast ads, text ads, shopping cart ads, telephone pole ads, storefront ads, garbage can ads, washroom ads, bus shelter and subway ads, robo calls, street ads, and any other place some enterprising ad profession has thought of, it's not hard to believe.

Now add to this the number of text messages, e-mails, social posts, direct messages, and even telephone calls we get over the course of the day. It's no wonder, so many of us just want to unplug and disconnect. We are walking receivers of thousands of people and brands who just want our attention.

Real life "Mad Men" ad pro, Howard Luck Gossage once wrote that: "People don't read ads. They read what interests them. Sometimes it's an ad." Most of us survive well against this barrage of artillery fire to the point of being oblivious to the distractions of our day-to-day lives.

Observers say social media has changed everything. In marketing. In branding. In spreading the word. In human connections.

News and information used to be disseminated through media houses from newspapers to television. Now we rely on Dr. Google, Twitter, Reddit, and any other forum and platform to seek our own information. Now anyone can be a powerhouse of broadcasting information or misinformation. To recall Marshall Mcluhan[1], the medium is the message. Possibly. But the message is still the message regardless of the media carrying it. Messages are at its most fundamental still a story, that if engaging enough transcends

---

[1] Media theorist and professor known for his studies of mass media thought and behavior.

the medium carrying it. The medium is where it can be amplified. It's the carrier of your message and ultimately your brand. Understanding how messages are conveyed to the public is key to making your brand a reality.

Over the years, I have heard this from clients: "Everyone is on Facebook/Twitter/Instagram/TikTok (or _____), shouldn't we be there?" While these are standard platforms, the guiding rule is to be where your audience is. Each media platform has its own defined set of demographics and audience profile. And there are even subgroups segments within that. Soccer moms who are into recipe sharing. Vegans who are bodybuilders. College guys who are gaming enthusiasts. Know your audience and go where they go is the guide.

Looking to connect with CEOs? Perhaps, LinkedIn. Connecting with fashion enthusiasts? Instagram. Home decor, perhaps Pinterest. EV drivers? Perhaps, special interest forums. The challenge for most of us is keeping up with the Kardashians.

For every successful personality who has 100 million followers, there are multiples of aspiring influencers with their own little tribe of thousands or hundreds of followers or less.

Political aspirations? Look for those groups that can get you started—ratepayers, community interest groups, and club crowds. It's all about establishing your initial fan base.

For most of us in career mode, LinkedIn or other professional organizations are media to be known among our peer group.

The reason we focus on more finely tuned target groups is because of that large number of messages we are bombarded with on a daily basis. Being on the latest social media platform just because everyone else is on it could mean simply you're one of many, many voices vying for attention.

There are two points to be made here. You need to be relevant and you need to target people who matter most. Quality over quantity unless you're a mass brand. The media we have at our disposal is so finely divided that we no longer need to reach millions to get to our thousands or hundreds or dozens of our key targeted people. We can go to our selection of people much more directly.

Within these platforms, look at your profile. Each platform typically lets you post a photo and a summary. Does your photo reflect the brand personality we talked about earlier? Does it reflect the story you're looking to tell?

Does your summary hit the emotional hot button, get across your narrative, your key message? If not, refine, edit, and fix it.

To Tagline or Not to Tagline

"Make America Great Again" (MAGA). While popularized by Donald Trump, the phrase was used first by Ronald Reagan in his own 1980 presidential campaign. There it was first a line in a speech and then on campaign merchandise. Pundits have said, the only thing Trump came up with was the story that he created the phrase. Though not created by Trump, by trademarking and using it pervasively, it became his tagline. True, but by repeating it over and over, and placing it in caps on caps, it became his line and the slogan that entered the American consciousness.

And in an "if you don't control the story, someone else will" scenario, the MAGA line has been embodied by as far right as you can go as standing for Confederate bent views.

In another appropriation of sorts, "That's hot," the sit-com like phrase was not actually invented by Paris Hilton, but trademarked by her. She of the "Simple Life" reality TV celebrity and hotel socialite fame who built an enterprising enterprise around being famous just for being famous. Not only did she fan the flames of fame with the line, but she was also able to monetize it and keep others from doing so.

Similarly, in situations like quarterback baller, Tom Brady who tried to trademark Tom Terrific, it was not a way of monetizing it. But as a way of preventing other people from doing so.

From the world of big company brands, a tagline is the summation of their point of difference in the marketplace. And it works well when millions of dollars are spent placing it well in the minds of consumers.

One line, that has an enduring beauty to it, is Debeers'. Although I wasn't part of the team or in the room when the line was created, I imagine the work that went into it may have initially been expressed differently. Writing up the long form may have read like this: "A diamond is the hardest substance on earth that is a beautiful symbol of eternal love." Much more plodding than the deeper, "A diamond is forever." The expression of love is implicit and built into the words. If a diamond is forever, so too is my love with a Debeers diamond.

For personal taglines, it's a summation of all that you are. You've done your six words. Does it become your tagline? Sometimes. If well-written, it can be used as your personal tagline but think of that exercise as your content and the actual tagline writing as the tone and manner in which you bring it to life.

Which brings us back to our initial question: do we create a personal slogan or not? Should you use it? Entire seminars are run to help you write this personal brand line, but how important is it? For every memorable line, there are thousands more that are easily forgettable and mean little to the public.

To my clients, I have often advised using the tagline internally for their staff and team to get behind a common thought. It gives them a battle cry, an expression of their purpose. They have a better understanding and connection to the words than the general public. So, too with our personal brand.

Few of us have the skill and deft to create lines that enter into the minds of the public that it becomes an expression, let alone a trending meme. So, think of taglines as quick expressions to help you focus your brand story but it will be the deeper story that will resonate with your audience.

For politicians and personalities, if you have a catchphrase and you want to monetize it, trademarking is often the course. During Republican nominations of a previous voter year, other candidates such as Ted Cruz tried to own Make America Great Again. But someone else had the copyright. With ownership established, Donald Trump prevented others from using it. I suspect even Ronald Reagan would have been thwarted from coining it as well. For a mere $325 registration fee, Trump squatted on its use and got returns million times over from it.

For your own brand, start with the meaning and the story behind it and then look. If there may be a commercial opportunity, then look into trademarks.

CHAPTER 22

Building a Fanbase

In marketing, we refer to as creating brand advocates. But a simpler word is a fan. Someone who sings your praises. Colleague. Client. Customers.

What if I don't have any, you ask. That my friend is the work you do on yourself. Identify what is lacking. Building the skills, the character. And then come back to this.

If you're looking to build a social media presence, it's not just announcing to the world that you're there. It's being able to provide value to your potential fanbase.

What is it that you can offer people? Advice. Insights. Entertainment. Photos of your meals on Instagram aren't enough. What value are you providing?

And sometimes, all it takes is one strong advocate.

There was a YouTube video shot at the Sasquatch music festival in 2009. It's the story of one lone shirtless guy dancing out in the middle of a field that spurred on a major dance party. With over 21 million views, it's the perfect illustration of how it just takes one fan to start a movement. The principle is that it's not the leader but the first follower who spurred others to action and created a genuine follow-the-guy-next-to-the-leader movement.

Every fanbase starts with its first fan. Often, brand loyalty begins with the early adopters. In people brands, it's more aligned to your immediate circle. More than cheerleaders, but people who would go to bat for you. Who would be willing to take the risk. The second guy in the dance video is the one taking the risk. While the first dancer is the don't-really-care-what-others-think kind of guy. It's the second one who takes the bigger risk because he's chosen to be the I-believe-in-him kind of person.

While the dancefest movement was spurred by the follower, it truly was the first dancer who inspired the second guy to follow. If the first dancer didn't have his own passion and belief; if he gave up, there'd be no dance video. But he kept at it. That passion and belief inspired another. Building a fanbase starts with that steadfast belief.

One of the ultimate personal brands is Jesus Christ. Where would the Christian movement be without his disciples, his brand advocates (save for Judas) spreading his beliefs? But his first influencer was John who brought along his own disciples.

Referencing another religious term, epiphanies aren't so much an awakening but a reinforcement of your core beliefs. Ever heard a statement and you go "yeah, that's me" in reaction to hearing a story. It's not a shift in what you believe but a reinforcement of what you know inside to be true.

A colleague was telling me about Spanx and its untold popularity. Being the male of the species, I had to Google the church of Spanx to understand this unique product. From Sara Blakely, the billionaire founder of Spanx in her Masterclass lecture, "The more vulnerable you're willing to be, the deeper the connection will be with the consumer." Tummy and other body part tucking is deeply personal and sharing it, even more so. The brand of Spanx was built on the personal endorsements of the likes of Oprah Winfrey and others.

This is where your purpose comes into play. If you can open yourself up, articulate it, and share it, people who align with it will get behind it.

Who are the genuine cheerleaders in your life? Those emissaries who can help carry your idea, your brand. While starting a religious movement is not your focus, having supporters can propel your brand forward.

While you may not have an ardent base of fans yet, you can start the movement. It can be as simple as collecting testimonials from colleagues. Having them give you a LinkedIn endorsement. Sharing testimonials of people also gives permission for others to believe the same.

Donald Trump, the once populist president, had a Twitter fanbase and audience that swelled to well over 88 million people. Although the account has since been removed, there will always be ardent believers. But that mass outer circle has disappeared. The one takeaway in a postgame analysis is that Trump with his followers had his own audience. He did not need to rely on traditional media to get his message out. He had his own media platform.

Know that having an audience doesn't make you an influencer. It makes you a media platform. Like a magazine, you have a circulation of potential readers. A circulation of 1 million people doesn't mean you can influence them; it means you have an audience. That said, personalities, Kim and Kylie Kardashian are true influencers. They say something, and people will react and jump on their recommendations.

Influencing people begins with the immediate group of people whom you affect. Who can be your advocates. Who will align with you? It begins with you believing in what you believe in. Standing for something.

CHAPTER 23

Taking Your Brand
to Market

Expressing your brand in the public eye. This is where the media hits the road. Survey what you have currently. Let's look at the tools that are available. Instagram, TikTok, YouTube, Clubhouse, Caffeine, and others that not only dizzy the mind but no doubt more as this book is published.

It matters not. That same principle applies. Go where your audience is.

There are foundational items that as a brand you may want to have.

Personal website. LinkedIn profile. Personal social media to show an added dimension to your brand persona. Be open to other tools if LinkedIn or Facebook don't provide enough of a forum to tell your story. People in my business have an online portfolio—a curated collection of their work.

And this is the perfect time to take a look at your resume or CV. With countless online guides available, putting together a CV isn't a difficult task. Nor is a shortage of techniques and workarounds that ensure your resume gets past the recruitment bots.

The only thing I will add to the advice column is to ensure that you include a narrative. At some point, a real human being will review your resume. What is the story that you are trying to tell? What is the connection you are looking to make?

The reason most of us head to social media is the magic word, free. It's often the reason our clients push for it. For some, the stars align and their story on a social media platform takes off and collects hundreds of thousands if not millions of followers. The appeal is there. Set up a SnapChat/Twitch/Instagram/TikTok and voila, you not only gain thousands of followers, you might even be an influencer.

The reality is the effort that goes into stimulating engagement with people to gain and retain followers. This is work. And it may be all sweat equity. Or, it may be on a brand level, paid resources—to not only create content but to push it. Brands pay professionals or hire social media specialists to create the content, writing, shooting, video recording, and polishing each post. It's not enough to simply create content, you have to distribute it, push it out, and get it out in front of enough eyeballs that will engage and hopefully buy into your brand.

Let's look at some of the astronomical numbers for Instagram celebrities:

Cristiano Ronaldo (441 million followers)

Kylie Jenner (337 million followers)

Dwayne 'The Rock' Johnson (315 million followers)

Ariana Grande (310 million followers)

And on and on. Like a baseball scorecard, these will change as each famous person jockeys for position, but here's the point. Unless you're a celebrity or personality who has a built-in audience, hyper jumping to these numbers does require resources.

Paying to boost your posts, creating content to keep your account active all require time, resources, and money. Interesting and perhaps ironically, I've kept off social media for this reason. So, has much of my team. Like the shoemaker's children, we spend more time helping brands that we have little energy or desire to socialize within social media.

This is as true for many who have gone on this track. Many find too much work in sustaining their presence. The goal of doing social shouldn't be to gain followers but the outcome of expressing your brand. The followers are the by-product of you connecting to your tribe.

In marketing and PR, there is paid media and earned media.

Earned media is getting your story covered by a third party from newspaper and TV media outlets through to podcasts without having to pay for the privilege. The financial investment may be minimal but the time resource investment can be greater. There is no such thing as a free lunch, as 19th-century industrialist John Ruskin said.

Speaking engagement: You invest your time to create a talk that you deliver at a conference or within an organization. For some, the return on this can be worthwhile when they are paid to speak.

Podcast: You invest time to appear on narrow casted audio or video only.

Articles: You invest time to write an article on your area of expertise that is published on a media platform. Sometimes paid and sometimes just to have your professional persona made credible. You will see this in the business section of newspapers where an accountant, lawyer, or expert is able to dispense their wisdom.

Press release: You invest time to write about your endeavor, your book, your idea and you send out to media publications and platforms in hopes that it will be picked up as news or gain a response that can lead to an interview for an article or show. You can send it out yourself to said media outlets. You can find a section on most of their websites that allow you to submit a story idea. You can also pay a distribution service such as Business Wire which sends out your press releases to hundreds of news media, information websites, bloggers, and even social networks.

Books: You invest time in putting your expertise or thought leadership onto paper or Kindle.

One on one: You invest time with individuals. Sales people and politicians are all too familiar with the act of campaigning and shaking hands in this one-on-one approach to getting their brand out there.

Paid media is bought. As simple as that. And there's no shortage of options available to you. Some brief highlights, because if you can put a message on it (recalling public toilets and coasters, waitresses' t-shirts at the pub the other night), you can sell it as an advertising medium.

Advertising: From local ads for real estate agents to full-page newspaper ads or on a more controlled level digital ads in the form of Google or Facebook ads, you pay to have your message put out the platform or media outlet's audience.

Boosted social posts: You pay to have posts seen by more people, broadly or targeted.

Sponsored content: You pay to have an article written about you or your brand.

TV airtime: You pay for a block of time on air. Many local business people and personalities in your cities have them. A person whose ego is as big as their wallet buys a half hour or hour slot on the local TV station and runs their own talk show showcasing their own space.

Public relations: You pay professionals to make connections to broad-based media.

This is by no means a comprehensive list of media available to you. With all of this, before you decide where you pay for the media or invest your labor in participating in a form of earned media, look at the audience size and profile. It's a good way to compare the choices available to you. Can't decide between a magazine ad or boosting your social media post. Compare the circulation size or the number of projected impressions. This is the number of people you can potentially reach. How do they compare against each other? Further, are they the target or can they influence the target of your personal brand?

Make Outreach a Habit

Posting, engaging, and connecting with your followers requires time and attention. Because for many, it's an extracurricular activity beyond your day job that requires committing to it. So, work out a plan. Intent and committing to it are two different things. Commit to a plan, or it just won't happen. Post one a week. Write an article one a month. Connect with people every other day. It doesn't matter as long as you stick to a plan that ensures it gets done. As a creative person, discipline isn't a habit people in my industry typically follow. That's why we've always had account and project managers to babysit us to deliver to deadlines. Structure a schedule. And once you get into the habit, it becomes rote. I wrote this book devoting every Saturday morning to writing. Some days more successful than others. But, it inched along. And, it can for you.

CHAPTER 24

Network Like a Brand

Everyone understands networking. It's all about connecting with others so that you have a base of valuable people with whom you can do business with or can help you in your career.

People often believe you need to be an extrovert with such an outgoing personality that others will want to hire you or do business with you. That you have to have such a dynamic personality that everyone wants to be part of your circle.

Think of networking in a different way. In life, many of us are not the life of the party, or the center of everyone's universe. We may be shy or introverted. But that doesn't mean you can't network and be successful.

Good strong brands aren't always the most lavish or in your face. Good brands (such as your favorite car or your favorite drink) don't try to sell you once, or look for what they can extract out of you in that quick exchange. Brands want an ongoing lasting relationship. To do that, they try to form a long-term relationship. They want you to share your experience with your friends. They want you to be the first thing you think of when you are shopping. They want you as a customer for life.

Let me share some insights from brands that can help you with networking. It's one simple thought: It's not about what people can do for you; it's about the benefit you can give to others.

Understand there are two types of relationships: Transactional ones, that are often based on price. And deep loyal relationships that are based on value.

The first offers little loyalty. It's fleeting. People who are your customers for this reason will move at the drop of a dollar. And people who are only in your network for your own benefit are like a shallow well that you try to draw from.

Customers and clients with whom you have a meaningful relationship will endeavor to help you, to do business with you, or introduce you to people who can assist you.

So, how do you get to that deeper relationship? By building social capital. Building social capital means contributing and helping others in their goals. It means creating a network where people want to help you because you want the same for them.

When I started my new firm a number of years ago, I realized this. I had enough social capital to establish a client base that got me going from day one. I was fortunate. But, it was based on the network I had built up over time.

Think of your favorite brand again. You have a high level of loyalty toward it. That's the beauty of a brand relationship. If it's a true relationship and not a transactional one, the bond between customer and brand can be so strong, they won't give up on it, no matter what. Forge relationships. Be that loved brand.

While your aim may be to gain a customer for life, the goal should be more to create a foundation for that type of relationship. The goal is to build up goodwill and capital that can assist you later in the form of a referral, an introduction, or even information. All valuable in the building of your network and your business success.

So, the next time you are networking or meeting people, don't just hand them your business card and hope that you can sell them (your product/service). Find out about their interests and business. Be genuinely interested and see how you might be able to help them with their pursuits. They may not provide you business. Truth is, it may not come back to help you. On the other hand, you've helped others. And isn't that our objective in life? To have friendships and relationships of permanence?

CHAPTER 25

Pitching Investors

I've been on both sides of initial investor meetings. An equity firm comes out to the company to meet the management team, take a tour, and poke around the factory as much as the accounting books. That first meet and greet and how you shape their imagination with your vision can be the difference between yay and nay.

This chapter reviews how to put your best sneaker encased foot forward.

I can't say I'm an expert in the area of investor relations the way financial consultants in this area are. I have however participated in a multitude of meetings, plant tours, wine tastings, all the while, presenting on behalf of my clients. The investors, whether equity, or private investors or banks, all have different areas of focus that are important to them.

Sometimes it's the finances, sometimes the operations, and sometimes the marketing side. There are pitch meetings, where as the marketing or brand "guru," I'm the main course for the investors. And to them, the highlight of the meeting. In other meetings, I have little relevance to them. So, I'm the attentive guy in a suit jacket quietly sitting in the corner.

They'd rather hear from the finance person.

No matter what the focus of the meeting, it's still the initial introduction by the founder of the company that not only sets the tone and direction of the meeting, but provides that opportunity to share their vision. It's the way the story is told that connects with the audience and hopefully pulls them into the CEO's orbit. And that's often my work behind the scenes: Creating and fine tuning the story.

If you've watched "Shark Tank," you recognize that those first 30 seconds are the most important to connecting with the investors and their financial resources.

It comes back to the story.

Nowhere is the 30 second or elevator pitch more needed than in these pitches. For those who may not be familiar with the term elevator pitch, think of that very scenario. You have the time it takes for the elevator to go from the time you enter to when it opens up to tell your story.

I have a friend, Michael, who once worked for a film editing company, the one of dozens of services that support the making of a movie. One day the office was abuzz with talk. Famed *Inception* and Tenet film director Christopher Nolan was coming in to oversee the cut of one of his films. My friend, a budding filmmaker, knew that there was no way he could approach him to pick his brain about his film secrets without getting shooed away. He did know that at 3:15 pm, Christopher Nolan would be moving from edit suite A to edit suite B. If he timed his coffee break at that time and happen to be walking down the same hallway at 3:15 pm, he could intercept the director, say hello, introduce himself, and casually ask him about his secrets to success. Like a well-planned heist movie, Michael's timing was perfect. His 30 seconds turned into an inspirational ten minutes of meaningful chit chat with the star director.

The initial story is just the beginning of a much more meaningful discussion and hopefully a relationship and a financial arrangement.

The initial meet and greet. If you have ever participated in a speed date, where with one-minute sessions, you go through a cycle of potential mates, you know the importance of getting the pitch right. Whether a fintech conference or personal networking, your story is also your pitch.

The pitch deck. These do follow a common format.
Company Overview
Mission/Vision of the Company
The Team
The Market Situation and Problem
The Market Opportunity
The Solution
The Product
The Customers
The Technology
The Competition
Traction
Business Model

The Marketing Plan
Financials
The Ask

If you've never put one together, you can find many templates online to assist you. But don't just fill in the blanks. Each slide is an opportunity to imbue with your story in both a visual or verbal way.

What isn't on the slides is the "about you" and your journey you lace in and create the connection to your prospect. As the business leader, it's your story and the style of storytelling of your brand that can ignite the room and inspire confidence and belief in your leadership.

CHAPTER 26

How to Be a Cult Brand

When we think cults, we think of a nefarious group that recruits you, cajoles you, and ultimately controls you. We think of the likes of Jimmy Jones, of NXIVM, of charismatic leaders who control your mind, body, sometimes finances, and even soul. There is a slavish devotion and love of that leader.

We hear this term, but in reality, there is nothing evil, only success, about a product that reaches cult-like status. It's often the goal of many aspirational brands to reach this slave devotion. Who else but a marketing person must have coined the term. Such brands as Nike, Apple, and Tesla, typically, have an engaging and at times charismatic leader or surrogate (in the form of a spokesperson or brand ambassador) who sees the world differently (see Steve Jobs and Elon Musk).

The competition often thought of as the enemy is clearly laid out before the audience (the establishment typically). Remember the Mac versus PC. And now Tesla vehicles versus the GMs and Fords of the world. They appeal to the early adopters who are willing to give up more of their money to be different from everyone else. Apple computers, to this day, and the first wave of Model Ss and Model Xs are priced at a premium level.

The key aspect that I've observed in the making of a cult brand is the satisfaction of being different. Being embraced for the elements of your personality that you are.

An epiphany is defined as a sudden realization or revelation. We often think of it as the "aha" moment in which your belief system is shaken. In my observation, an epiphany is more an affirmation of something you have always believed in deep down inside but could never articulate as well. By appealing to the misfits and the outcasts, Apple taught us it was okay to "Think Different." The company did not go after the masses at first; they went after those who had a desire to be accepted in their own way. While masses were content living the status quo with beige computer boxes, press button cell phones, Apple truly thought differently.

Back then, Apple represented a minor segment of any of their tech markets in computing, telecommunications, music, and entertainment. They are not only one of the world's largest companies, but also the world's largest companies by market capitalization. And the most profitable company. My investment portfolio thanks you. And this from a company that at first didn't appeal to the broad masses now appeals to the broad masses.

To help you understand how you can derive some of the learnings of how brands become cults, let's look at the practical elements of a cult.

A leader who is often charismatic. They have firm beliefs. They fulfill a need that people are missing themselves, often love and a sense of belonging. This leads to early adopters. They need to communicate well.

Raëlism is a following, which is sometimes described as a religion based on UFOs. Started and led by a French auto journalist named Claude Vorilhon in the 1970s. The philosophy ascribes to a belief that we are all descended from ancient alien space travelers. Now the belief system is not so far fetched as it might seem. A survey by *National Geographic* found that 77 percent of Americans think that aliens have visited the Earth.

While not everyone can be a cult leader, we can look at what makes a cult brand and the ingredients used to create that undying loyalty among your advocates.

You don't need to be charismatic, but you should strongly believe in your purpose to the point of passion. Infamous cult leaders such as Charles Manson and Jimmy Jones didn't have a huge Christian-like following, but they did have a zealous view of their philosophy.

What need can you fulfill? While you may argue the validity of these out-there beliefs, history has shown us, if you deliver your message fervently enough and strong enough, there will be people who will agree and follow you. Hitler, and other dictators, prove that passion can be infectious and lead to incitement.

In the late 90s, when I worked for Saatchi & Saatchi, worldwide CEO Kevin Roberts introduced the concept of a Lovemark, the idea of attaching a very strong emotion to a brand. While his implosion over sexist remarks colors his career, his principle is still an interesting and valid one to look at.

Though some marketers question the usefulness of the Lovemarks concept, the concept of having great attachment to a brand can be found in top populist brands. It's very much a relationship of love.

While Nike can be considered a lovemark, it was a cult brand before becoming a pop brand. But it's the core group in the beginning that are loyal, loyal followers. That first ring of people who are undying lovers of the brand in which it can do no wrong. Very much like a romantic relationship. At the beginning, when love first takes hold with that special someone, the focus is only on you. You feel special and unique like you're the most important person in the world. But if the love of your life loves everyone else, and everyone loves them, you may not feel that special relationship anymore. Not ideal for us as emotional creatures. But for brands appealing to the masses, profit and success are exactly what they were looking for.

The Beatles phenomenon of the 1960s supports a fanatical love of musical brand. Girls fainting, screaming, deciding who was their favorite Beatle, who they were going to marry was part of this undying loyalty.

At the height of love, people will risk all with a die-for-you type of loyalty and provide an envied brand worship. Or at the very least, the next love comes along.

Entities whether brands or people provide that a crucial second element: A need fulfilled.

You also need to communicate your beliefs or your concepts well. Perhaps, it's no surprise that Claude Vorilhon or Scientology founder, L. Ron Hubbard were writers. It's often the communication oratory skills or stage presence that yields the power. And in as many instances, you may have a disciple(s) who can do it on your behalf.

Remember the dance video I wrote about earlier, where one dancer, one follower became the spark to follow the leader. It's the emissaries who become your influencers, those who follow. Disciples. A core group of followers can lead to a massive throng.

These can be your employees, your squad, and your department, who follow you based on the (cult)ure you build. Fact is for many companies, it's the employees who live and breathe your brand that help to provide those emissaries.

To understand the power of this, look at when the opposite is true. You encounter a product brand through advertising or social media. You get excited about it but when you call up or visit the store, the people behind the counter provide such a bad or opposite impression, you are turned off and decide never to buy that brand again. We used to see that a lot in the car business. The brand versus showroom experience.

Making your employees your evangelists is key. They are your second or third and fourth dancers.

Creating a cult relationship isn't about being everything to everyone. After all, while 74 million people voted for Trump, 81 million did not. And Gwenneth Paltrow and her Goop philosophy has her haters. It's about pronouncing your traits. People gravitate to you based on similar traits and beliefs.

It's the basis of human relationships. Why do relationships fail? In life, especially dating, common interests are no basis for sustaining a deep relationship. You both may like comedy or motorsports, but any relationship doomed for success relies on common values. It's not enough to simply like the same things (this is a superficial transaction of sorts).

Your immediate followers are those who have similar values, they have or want the same mission in life. The outer ring is there because they have the same interests but will fall away at the first sign of scandal, because the relationship is merely transactional. So, understand your traits, your strengths, and most importantly, what you believe in.

This book isn't meant for you to become a cult leader but by understanding the thinking, you can certainly be more than one of the masses.

CHAPTER 27

On Reputation

Here is a template of a PR announcement: "Following our internal review of the incident in yesterday, we have made the decision to terminate the employee involved, effective immediately. We do not tolerate racism of any kind at."

I was about to share a story. But it's so familiar that the location could be anywhere and the organization, any company.

An individual confronts a person of color, it's recorded, and it makes the news. Sometimes it's seemingly a person trying to be funny, although with no hate bias but is still considered racist.

"Going to Africa. Hope I don't get AIDS. Just kidding. I'm white!"

In the multihour flight that Justine Sacco took following her tweet, she was vilified by the public and quickly fired by her employer by the time she landed.

"The offensive comment does not reflect the views and values of IAC. We take this issue very seriously, and we have parted ways with the employee in question." This could be supplied as a familiar template for any damage control PR release

Ricky Gervais among others writes that "reputation is what strangers think of you, and character is who you really are."

I once had a person of a public organization come to me. He was in a not unfamiliar situation. He was outed for having a much more personal relationship with a younger worker in his organization. His texts were exposed for the world to see. He was married. In the end, I couldn't really help him. There was little to salvage or change the narrative. He was unrepentant, unwilling to take responsibility, and more focused on the conspiracy theory that the media was out to get him. While no judgement, his character was exactly what people perceived of him. There was little to build on.

What should you do when your brand implodes? Understand first, it's what happens when one's persona doesn't align with your brand. If Tiger Woods was more a bad boy and it being the reason for his brand success, his scandal in 2009 would have been a minor story. Instead, his was one of the carefully crafted-story of an American boy who rose up in a long-time Establishment sport. As a rapper, his dalliances would have helped his reputation. As a golfer where race runs a thin line of tolerance, it was easy to vilify him.

Can you rebuild a brand, once trashed and tossed out by the public. You have to wonder if we have advanced as a society from the public floggings when convicted criminals were taken into a public square in shackles and punished while everyone looked on. At least those days, you may have had a day in court. Public scrutiny is both judge and executioner rolled in one.

Social media is truly citizen journalism. Of the people by the people. Not of news credibility but of news sharing. Act up in public, and a video is shot and uploaded and shared.

So, what happens when the rumor mill overtakes your reputation? What happens when the rumor is stronger than the brand? Or, only provides part of the picture. If what the world believes is true, how can you counter that?

Perhaps, the most well-known story of a "Karen," a term given to a seemingly overprivileged white woman who complains about some perceived slight and captured on video, is that of Amy Cooper. Her "incident' of not wanting to leash her dog was in Central Park where she had an exchange with a bird-watching Black man, named Christian Cooper got her initially charged with making a false report, and as news reports and even a Wikipedia entry tell us, publicly shamed by anyone who had an opinion and fired by her employer, Franklin Templeton.

Her apology and initial retreat into the shadows was her reaction of accepting a level of responsibility, but also the story that was being told. That was, until it affected her financially. Her company dismissed her without severance and what may be owing her in the employer/employee agreement. Swinging back, Amy Cooper and her lawyer were suing for unspecified damages for race and gender discrimination, defamation, intentional infliction of emotional distress, and negligence. As news reports say, Cooper filed a criminal complaint against Franklin Templeton claiming that her employer fired her without investigating the incident. She also claimed that Franklin Templeton falsely portrayed her as racist, and that Christian Cooper was an "overzealous birdwatcher" who had selected her as a "target."

Her story is being told by her lawyers, a medium, by which carries a certain hammer-like authority. Whether you agree with her or not, whether you believe her or not, managing your brand reputationally means inserting, or countering the narrative with your own. And as the public once again takes sides, in the world of brands, the truth is what people believe to be true.

To help play it out to your side, look at the key brand attribute. Is the reason to believe there? Can it be substantiated?

Ultimately, being preemptive is best. If your brand and reputation is established, it becomes much more difficult to move people off that belief.

Most of us will not suffer the delighted schadenfreude of seeing our demise. We may, however, have a negative review or comment on one of our posts. Or have an old post come back to bite us. It's the digital footprint few of us can escape from. I have had clients who hired firms in India to submit positive reviews either to bolster their online reputation or to push down or offset negative reviews that exist on Google.

While I am neutral on such practices, Google does have tools to help you manage some of your public presence. Outdated info such as old web pages, you'd like to jettison. Perhaps, it's a membership in a club that may not be aligned with the values of your new company. While the page has been removed, the information still shows up when you Google your name. It means an old version of the page is still cached on Google's servers. You can submit the URL to Google to have them remove it. And for fake or falsely negative reviews, you can report this too to Google for removal as well.

Last year, I was observing how the number one celebrity chef, Gordon Ramsay, began acting as pitchman for Silk Oat Beverage, a plant-based, vegan-friendly milk replacement. This coming from a man who has trolled and punked vegans and has said, "If the kids ever came up to me and said, 'Dad, I'm a vegetarian,' then I would sit them on the fence and electrocute them."

But to make his endorsed position credible, I imagine that his brand advisors did do something smart. They pumped out a press release announcing how he was going to the bright side embracing more of plant-based cuisine. He even joked to his more than 11 million followers that "I've got a confession. After three decades of cooking, hundreds and hundreds of thousands of hours behind the stove I … I'm turning vegan." And then, the punchline, "For lunch only." But it was enough to set the stage for another carefully crafted story that was released weeks before his Silk Oat endorsement. It was one that talked about the impact of his kids having a strong influence on his shift in diet and cooking. It had all the perfect elements of carefully measured believability (healthier) and sincerity (family) to change the narrative and set the stage for Silk Oat.

In branding, if what is being said doesn't align with your brand, you change the conversation. If you don't like the narrative, manage it.

But we all make mistakes. To err is human. Until the public view swings to one of a more compassionate culture rather than a cancel culture, it's one we have to contend with. And while each situation varies, the stronger your brand, the more it can eclipse a potential bad reputation.

Changing and managing the narrative is a key part of it. PR experts who manage clients who have fallen often stick to a tried and true game plan that seems to be as much a page out of Alcoholics Anonymous's 12-step program as it is of PR guidebook.

- Sincerely demonstrate remorse and take responsibility for your actions
- Make amends with the people you have wronged
- Seek to rebuild trust with your target group

We have seen it work for likes of domestic queen Martha Stewart but less so for outed cycling cheat Lance Armstrong. The latter who denied so hard and for so long, his new narrative couldn't offset it.

And in the end, no amount of controlling the narrative can offset a crime and monstrous act. The reason to believe has to be there. And it does begin with a strategy to manage it.

CHAPTER 28

What to Do When Your Brand Goes Stale

If you saw a little alligator emblem on a polo shirt, you would instantly recognize it as being a Lacoste, the hugely popular fashion brand. What you may not know is the story of how René Lacoste who won 10 Grand Slam tennis tournaments almost 100 years ago started a fashion. It was hugely popular through the 80s so much so that it was seen everywhere. Chinese counterfeiters even began knocking it off and could be found in the back alleys of Canal Street in New York. Ubiquity was also its temporary downfall. If you ever enjoyed the mangled aphorisms of baseball icon, Yogi Berra, you'd understand what he meant when he described a popular restaurant with the pithy observation of "Nobody goes there anymore. It's too crowded." So, too was Lacoste. In addition to its business split with Izod, the brand's popularity had waned. New design and brand attitude began to restore its elite status and brand popularity.

If fashion brands are a good lesson for all brands, look to another cautionary tale of Tommy Hilfiger. Hilfiger was once such a strong brand among the urban crowd and celebrities including music superstars like Michael Jackson. As they broadened and expanded, trying to diversify into women's fashions with bath products and cosmetics, it too began losing its way by the aughts. In interviews, Hilfiger admitted to trying to stay on trends the demand failed to live up to the mass supply. Discounting and reducing price (as we know from the importance of brand value) did little as sales began sinking. Quality had to be compromised to allow for cheaper prices. Consumers lost faith, but to maintain this cycle, the company had to continue to sell cheaper goods at cheaper prices. And that children, is how the Hilfiger label lost its brand value.

Like unwanted guests, brands can overstay their welcome. As important as dealing with when your reputation overtakes your brand is when your brand goes stale. When it's been around a little too long.

Let's talk about how to take a defibrillator to your brand. Go back to the beginning of the process, take stock, and do an audit. See where your skill sets are where it has or can evolve. We look at where your key attributes are, where it was, or how it can evolve. If you were popular once, what was the essence that got you there?

What resonates with your audience? The key word, being, your audience. The point of not trying to be everything to everyone is clear.

Nowhere is this more seen than in the world of politics. An elected official will have gained enough votes to take office but never have they shut out their opponent. When was the last time you remember an elected politician's opponent getting zero votes? In theory, politicians have their core stance that brings in hopefully for them enough popularity in their territory to win. Watering down their stance for wider appeal can mean not standing for anything worth voting for. Which is why we see such increasingly divisive views now in politics.

Next, we talk about re-establishing and rebranding.

CHAPTER 29

Re-Establishing +
Rebranding Yourself

Renovation Hardware used to be a hardware type store. It was founded in 1979 by Stephen Gordon, who while renovating his home couldn't find fixtures and traditional American hinges door knobs. It became a retail store where you could get little odd knick knacks. Retro metal toys like the space guns you would squeeze a trigger and little siren sounds would delight kids from long ago. Today, it's a showroom of expensive furniture where it would be unlikely you would find any tin toys.

The story of George Foreman is another such story. If you look back on early interview footage of this boxing great, especially when compared to the greatest and his greatest nemesis, Muhammad Ali, you will see a man then lacking the pitch perfect charisma of the man you see today.

In Toronto, in the downtown core, at the Times Square of the city, Yonge and Dundas stands the soapbox derbies of sermons. I once stood for a good 20 minutes watching a street preacher at the south-west corner by Toronto's Eaton Centre. A young man dressed in a fitting trench coat, stood and delivered a passionate sermon that he must have done week after week. I am convinced that the successful religious leaders know their marketing pitch: A key message with key takeaways, wrapped in a story that's delivered such conviction that they connect on a profound level with their audience.

Rev. George Foreman developed his pitch and his thunder, delivering sermons from week to week. After what Foreman described as a near-death express, he hung up the gloves until his comeback and became an ordained minister. He began preaching on street corners before becoming the reverend in Houston. No wonder he could sell electric grills on late-night TV.

At the height of her career, music icon Madonna was most known for her constantly changing image. Some saw it as a rebranding herself. But her brand was really built around being a chameleon as she morphed from her street punk look to her Voguing life to bondage apparel. It wasn't so much a rebrand as she stayed consistent with her outrageousness.

True rebrands are transformations as the story and narrative changes along with the shift. From Angelina Jolie shapeshifting from perceived bizarre behavior to elegant UN humanitarian. Robert Downey from drug addict to superhero. Controlled and fabricated, perhaps but well-accepted by the public where it's the most relevant.

But how about for us lesser celebrities? Is it possible to rebrand yourself? To change the public perception of yourself. Rebranding often means shifting the story to one that can connect better with your target market.

If you live up to that new image or one that is more consistent with the real you, the answer will be yes. Yes, you can create a new brand that may be more in line with a new direction and changes in your life.

Determine if the gap between who you are and what you want to be is narrow enough to shift. The wider the gap, more time and resources are needed to shift that perception. It's pressing a reset button of sorts. Reincarnating yourself. Follow the steps outlined here. Take stock of yourself. See where you are and where you want to be.

CHAPTER 30

Stay Consistent. Please

Clients I have worked with sometimes suffer the shiny bead syndrome. They see something bright and shiny and gravitate to it.

I once wrote a commercial for a large corporate company. Admittedly, it narrowly pushed the bounds of taste. It featured cannibals and other Saturday Night Live type humor that wasn't "on brand." Our words for saying it wasn't consistent with the brand. But it was funny and entertaining and potentially award-winning. Every level of client from the brand manager to the VP of marketing and sales had approved it. It was a funny idea that would have been immensely entertaining. We commissioned a film company to produce it with an A-level director to bring our vision to life. The client put the requisite money down to see it through. It just needed one final sign off from the CEO who hadn't been privy to any of the creative discussions that lead us to his insane solution. The day before the shoot, he reviewed the idea and script and axed it. The people who previously approved it, now disavowed it like a mission gone wrong. The money spent became a kill fee to cover the cost of the bookings and talent and crew. At the time, everyone at the ad agency was bitterly disappointed claiming the CEO didn't know good creative if it slapped him in the face. Looking back on it years later, I do know he stuck to the values that were consistent with how he saw the brand. It would have gained notice for the spot; but for the longer term view, it would not have been consistent with the brand.

There are even Brand Indexes which measure the strength of a brand against financial value, shareholder impact, consumer connection, and other criteria. In marketing, we love measuring everything, assigning scores, and rankings. Depending on which study or ranking you look at names like Nike, Apple, and Disney are bandied about.

We judge brands on trust, reliability but as important is authenticity. Do we believe what they promise to deliver on? Are they true to their promise?

Once you establish what your brand is all about, stay with it. You've come this far, to establish a brand essence of who you are and how you will express it, why detour at this point?

Zappos, the shoe retailer, says it well, "As we grow, our processes and strategies may change, but these 10 Core Values will remain the same." This is consistency.

It's often easy to be distracted and move to something trendy. Avoid the trap of shifting. If you have done the work and established your brand, you will see that a message of consistency is one that stays.

CHAPTER 31

To Thine Own Self Be True

When you think of authentic brands, what comes to mind?

Read beauty brand, Dove's mission from their website: "We believe beauty should be a source of confidence, and not anxiety. That's why we are here to help women everywhere develop a positive relationship with the way they look, helping them raise their self-esteem and realize their full potential."

Or, outdoor wear, Patagonia's short treatise: "We're In Business To Save Our Home Planet."

And then shoe company and one of the first online retailers, Zappos's:

1. Deliver WOW Through Service
2. Embrace and Drive Change
3. Create Fun and A Little Weirdness
4. Be Adventurous, Creative, and Open-Minded
5. Pursue Growth and Learning
6. Build Open and Honest Relationships With Communication
7. Build a Positive Team and Family Spirit
8. Do More With Less
9. Be Passionate and Determined
10. Be Humble

No matter how they express it, many of these brands are built on a defined culture and values. Authenticity comes from living and believing in their purpose. And this applies to personal brands as well. And perhaps, it needs to be simpler than that for us as people brands.

Here is a story from Grammy Award winning singer and musician Alicia Keys in her biography, *More Myself*. In it, she recounts this upsetting story in her life when she did a photo shoot for her first album. She felt "manipulated" and "objectified" by a photographer who was left alone and encouraged her to open her shirt and pull down her jeans. "My spirit is screaming that something is wrong, that this feels sleazy. But my protests, lodged in the back of my throat, can't make their way out. If I say no, what doors will be closed to me? I swallow my misgivings, tuck my thumb between the denim and my skin, and obey." Even though it's been said sex sells, Keys was "embarrassed" and "ashamed" when the magazine came out. She also wrote, "I swear that I'll never again let someone rob me of my power."

Essena O'Neill was an Australian teen like many who wanted fame and fortune. Her route was using Instagram, then only 5 years in existence, to showcase her dream lifestyle of what many of us see as privilege. Well, it wasn't really her lifestyle. It was manufactured. Each post, each photo was created with the intention of showing the best photos of her life. But she wasn't happy. "I was really lost. Instagram had just come out when I was 14, so from 14 to 19 that was my whole life—my social circle, my dating, it was just everything," she said in an interview in *The Daily Mail.* "I started seeing things that I didn't like in myself, and that was terrifying ... so I quit, because I wasn't happy." Then in 2015, she quit. She quit the platform in which she had over 600,000 followers. She quit her public persona, admitting to herself and the world, that her day-to-day life was spent obsessing over public image. She was being her authentic self, when she began deleting more than 2,000 pictures of herself. Ironically, with Essena, there are still fan-created accounts on Instagram showcasing her old photos. Essena changed her handle to "Social Media is Not Real" and began showing how each photo was an artificial reality, contrived to show the best side of herself. Ironically, or not so ironically, her authentic action gained her more fans, doubling her followers to 1 million, until she just shut down the account.

There are books of stories like this which highlight how going against your image has been shown to create unhappiness when it doesn't align with your authentic self.

I've also been asked if a personal brand can be created for dating and relationships. Can this be used for personal relationships? I'm not a dating coach but I will share one insight.

Too many of us try to be something we're not to appeal to the target audience (a mate). We lose an unsustainable amount of weight, we show a fake interest in activities, and we create an illusion. And while you can net your dream partner, are you being true to yourself?

My last thought is really a lesson of being happy. Why put on a persona that isn't true to yourself? If you followed the exercises to get to your positioning and key message, it should be authentic, genuine, and sincere. In the end, find that equilibrium that is true to yourself. Be who you stand for. To thine own self be true.

CHAPTER 32

Not the End,
Just the Beginning

I believe Albert Einstein said, "Everything should be made as simple as possible, but not simpler."

However, as comic book hero, Barry Allen (*The Flash*), says to Bruce Wayne in the movie, *Justice League*, "That feels like an oversimplification." But if I were to do a recap of this book broken down as simple guiding principles, it would look like this.

Brand Audit—To take stock of and know yourself.

Brand Insight—To understand where you fit in your world, job, and business.

Brand Target—To center on who the real audience is for your brand.

Brand Positioning—To determine how you can stand out from the crowd, your competition.

Brand Narrative—To tell your story to yourself.

Brand Messaging—To tell what you're all about in a concise way for the rest of the world.

Brand Dimension—To express who you are in either visually, words, or through a symbol.

Brand Media—To find the platforms or carriers for your brand message.

This book is meant to get you started. Simple but not. The steps are easy to understand but the work needs to be done. Enjoy the journey. And, begin with your own "Once upon a time."

References

"Wheel of Emotions." (iStock, credit Paola Vasquez Duran).

Adejobi, A. March 21, 2021. "Gordon Ramsay Fools Fans Into Thinking He's 'Turned Vegan' as He Makes Shocking Confession." Metro. https://metro.co.uk/2021/03/21/gordon-ramsay-fools-fans-into-thinking-hes-turned-vegan-as-he-makes-shocking-confession-14279544/

Blakely, S. n.d. Masterclass. www.masterclass.com/classes/sara-blakely-teaches-self-made-entrepreneurship

Buffett, J., and G. Taylor. 1977. Margaritaville. ABC Records.

Carnegie, D. 1936. How to Win Friends and Influence People. Simon & Schuster.

Charisma. 1972. Monty Python's Flying Circus, Monty Python's Previous Record.

Cullen, Z.B., and R. Perez-Truglia. June 2021. "The Old Boys' Club: Schmoozing and the Gender Gap." Harvard Business School, Working Paper.

Dove. www.dove.com/us/en/stories/about-dove/our-vision.html

Fritzon, K., N. Brooks, and S. Croom. 2019. Corporate Psychopathy: Investigating Destructive Personalities in the Workplace. Palgrave Macmillan.

Harari, Y.N. 2014. Sapiens: A Brief History of Humankind. Dvir Publishing House Ltd.

Harish, A. June 27, 2012. "UFOs Exist, Say 36 Percent in National Geographic Survey." ABCNews. http://abcnews.go.com/Technology/ufos-exist-americans-national-geographic-survey/story?id=16661311

Keys, A. 2020. More Myself. Flatiron Books.

Marshall, G. 1976. Laverne & Shirley. ABC.

MBTI® Basics—The Myers & Briggs Foundation. www.myersbriggs.org/my-mbti-personality-type/mbti-basics/

Mill Creek Entertainment. 1974–1979. Good Times.

Murphy, A., and L. House. November 16, 2019. "Where is Essena O'Neill now?" The Daily Mail. www.dailymail.co.uk/femail/article-7693543/Former-social-media-star-Essena-ONeill-23-returns-Instagram-four-year-hiatus.html

NBC Universal. 1990–1994. The Fresh Prince of Bel-Air.

Paramount Pictures. 1995. Braveheart.

Paramount Pictures. 2000. Mission: Impossible 2.

Patagonia. www.patagonia.com.au/pages/our-mission

Phillips, J., M. Love, S. McKenzie, and T. Melcher. 1988. Kokomo. Elektra.

Plutchik, R. 2003. Emotions and Life: Perspectives from Psychology, Biology, and Evolution. American Psychological Association.

Powers, J. 2016. WKW: The Cinema of Wong Kar Wai. Rizzoli.

Roberts, K. 2005. *Lovemarks: The Future Beyond Brands.* PowerHouse Books.

Spellberg, C. March 03, 2021. "Taylor Swift Fans Attack 'Ginny & Georgia' Star Antonia Gentry with Racist Comments Amid "Sexist Joke" Controversy." Decider.com. https://decider.com/2021/03/03/taylor-swift-fans-ginny-georgia-racism

Storey, K. March 18, 2019. "Why the Black Turtleneck Was So Important to Elizabeth Holmes's Image." Esquire. www.esquire.com/style/mens-fashion/a26836670/elizabeth-holmes-steve-jobs-black-turtleneck/

TBWA\Media Arts Lab. 2006. "Get a Mac." Apple.

The Enneagram Institute. The Enneagram Types. www.enneagraminstitute.com/type-descriptions

The Guardian. 2016. "Saatchi & Saatchi Boss Resigns Amid Sexism Row." www.theguardian.com/media/2016/aug/03/saatchi-saatchi-boss-kevin-roberts-resigns-amid-sexism-row

Thorndike, E. 1920. "Halo Effect, The Constant Error in Psychological Ratings."

Trump, D. 2016. "Make America Great Again." https://trademarks.justia.com/857/83/make-america-great-85783371.html

Warner Bros. Pictures. 2005. *Batman Begins.*

Warner Bros. Pictures. 2017. *Justice League.*

Warner Media. 1994–2004. *Friends.*

Weiner, M. 2007. *Mad Men.* AMC.

YouTube—Sasquatch Music Festival. 2009. "Guy Starts Dance Party." https://youtu.be/GA8z7f7a2Pk

Zappos. www.zappos.com/about/what-we-live-by

About the Author

Brand strategist, writer, designer, creative director, speaker, **Henry Wong** is the president and brand strategist of Vyoo (pronounced view), a branding and content company based in Toronto, Canada. He has guided small upstarts and SMEs to 500-level companies. His roots span over 25 years of senior positions in the advertising industry including being Sr. VP. creative director for global ad agency, Saatchi & Saatchi. It was in the agency world where he refined his knowledge and current methods. In addition to applying his award-winning mind to such clients as Toyota and Procter & Gamble, Henry has guided politicians, professional athletes, TV personalities, as well as CEOs with their personal brands.

Index

OTHER TITLES IN THE BUSINESS CAREER DEVELOPMENT COLLECTION

Vilma Barr, Consultant, Editor

- *Remaining Relevant* by Karen Lawson
- *Pay Attention!* by Cassandra Bailey and Dana M. Schmidt
- *Social Media is About People* by Cassandra Bailey
- *Burn Ladders. Build Bridges.* by Alan M. Patterson
- *Decoding Your STEM Career* by Peter Devenyi
- *A Networking Playbook* by Darryl Howes
- *The Street-Smart Side of Business* by Tara Acosta
- *Rules Don't Work for Me* by Gail Summers
- *Fast Forward Your Career* by Simonetta Lureti and Lucio Furlani
- *Shaping Your Future* by Rita Rocker
- *Emotional Intelligence at Work* by Richard M. Contino and Penelope J. Holt
- *How to Use Marketing Techniques to Get a Great Job* by Edward Barr
- *Negotiate Your Way to Success* by Kasia Jagodzinska
- *How to Make Good Business Decisions* by J.C. Baker
- *Ask the Right Questions; Get the Right Job* by Edward Barr
- *Personal and Career Development* by Claudio A. Rivera and Elza Priede
- *Your GPS to Employment Success* by Beverly A. Williams
- *100 Skills of the Successful Sales Professional* by Alex Dripchak

Concise and Applied Business Books

The Collection listed above is one of 30 business subject collections that Business Expert Press has grown to make BEP a premiere publisher of print and digital books. Our concise and applied books are for...

- Professionals and Practitioners
- Faculty who adopt our books for courses
- Librarians who know that BEP's Digital Libraries are a unique way to offer students ebooks to download, not restricted with any digital rights management
- Executive Training Course Leaders
- Business Seminar Organizers

Business Expert Press books are for anyone who needs to dig deeper on business ideas, goals, and solutions to everyday problems. Whether one print book, one ebook, or buying a digital library of 110 ebooks, we remain the affordable and smart way to be business smart. For more information, please visit www.businessexpertpress.com, or contact sales@businessexpertpress.com.